A SPECTRUM *of* LEGACIES

The Gifts You Leave for Your

Children and Community

A SPECTRUM
of LEGACIES

The Gifts You Leave for Your

Children and Community

MARK A. WEBER

Edited by Kathryn A. Bolinske

VSP VINTON STREET PRESS

This book is intended to provide general information about the topics included. It is sold with the explicit understanding that while Mark A. Weber is an attorney and Managing Member of Legacy Spectrum Advisor, LLC, neither he, the company nor the publisher is engaged by the reader to provide legal, accounting, financial, tax or any other type of expert assistance. If readers require assistance in any of these areas, they should seek the assistance and services of a competent professional.

The sole purpose of this book is to educate. The author and his affiliates assume no liability or responsibility to any person or entity with respect to any loss or damage caused, or alleged to be caused, directly or indirectly by the information contained in it.

If you choose not to be bound by the statements above, you may return this book to the publisher for a full refund (less handling charges).

Finally, the author makes liberal use of case studies and examples from his own practice. The names of individuals, companies and other identifying facts have been changed to protect the identities of those involved. Therefore, any resemblance to actual individuals is purely coincidental.

For information contact:
Mark A. Weber *MarkWeber@SpectrumOfLegacies.com*

A SPECTRUM
of LEGACIES

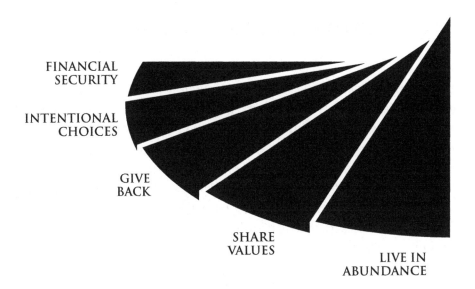

FINANCIAL
SECURITY

INTENTIONAL
CHOICES

GIVE
BACK

SHARE
VALUES

LIVE IN
ABUNDANCE

In *A Spectrum of Legacies* you will learn to:

1. **Achieve** lasting financial security;

2. **Make** intentional choices about how much of an inheritance to leave;

3. **Give** back to the community in a meaningful manner;

4. **Share** personal values with your children in the process of teaching them to responsibly handle money; and

5. **Live** the last part of your life in abundance.

Five-Star Reviews for
A Spectrum of Legacies
From Business Leaders, Academicians, and Professional Advisors

Since it was originally published, I have taught Mark Weber's **The Legacy Spectrum** *to hundreds of advisors and non-profit gift planners in the Chartered Advisor in Philanthropy designation at The American College of Financial Services. Consistently, students rate the book as the most valuable part of the curriculum. Distilling best practices into worksheets, Mark Weber equips readers to create a lasting legacy aligned with their values and ideals.* **A Spectrum of Legacies** *takes it to the next level with sample letters to children and trustees as well as definitive steps on how to make one's giving more impactful and rewarding.*

> Philip Cubeta, MSFS, CLU®, ChFC®, CAP®
> The Sallie B. and William B. Wallace Chair
>   in Philanthropy
> The American College of Financial Services

Mark Weber's work to help families plan for transferring wealth and values is extraordinary in a number of ways. Mark encourages a shared clarity within families that leads to better decisions and better relationships. He helps us understand that a plan which includes values frees both parents and children from the bounds of money and makes a better future possible for everyone involved—parents, children, and community. Finally, **A Spectrum of Legacies** *confirms the idea that money, once accumulated, until shared, has no value.*

> Mike McCarthy, Chairman
> Bridges Trust

A Spectrum of Legacies *provides a practical guide to the critical, and often missing, piece in wealth management and estate planning: a focus on meaning and values. Mark Weber's book is a practical and powerful guide with real world examples and compelling stories. It will make an important addition to the library of any planner or advisor.*

Russell N. James III, JD, PhD, CFP®
Director of Graduate Studies in
    Charitable Planning
Texas Tech University

A Spectrum of Legacies *is a gift to parents who care more deeply about the impact their financial wealth will have on their heirs and communities, than about the preservation of that capital. Mark Weber's gift not only generously provides inspiring stories, helpful worksheets, and sample letters, but helps both wealth creators and their advisors understand how important it is we not settle for the assumptions and limitations of traditional planning.* **A Spectrum of Legacies** *will take off the estate and legacy planning blinders we all wear and help us see the bright horizon of possibilities. Those who follow the suggestions Mark offers will find the path to creating meaningful and sustainable legacies.*

John A. Warnick, JD
Founder, The Purposeful Planning Institute

Until reading this book, I considered my legacy as passing on my knowledge based on my experience, education, training, and commitment to my profession. After reading this book, I realized I had too narrow of a definition of the legacy I wished to leave. My estate planning experience was indeed as described in the book, entirely focused on asset distribution and tax strategies. **A Spectrum of Legacies** *takes us to 'what's possible' as it pertains to passing along our assets, but also our values and greater insights of who we are and what is important to us and to those we love who will be the ultimate beneficiaries of our estate.*

Allen Fredrickson
CEO and President
Signature Performance

Weber is to be congratulated on another well-written book for those who work in the space and the rest of us trying to do the right thing and make an impact. He inspires the reader and provides a guide to find our own spectrum of legacies.

George Nichols III
President and CEO
The American College of Financial Services

Mark Weber has a passion for making the world a better place with a guidebook for helping people think about their values, their families, their money, and the legacy they want to leave behind. His passion borders on a ministry to help counsel people about the wealth they have and how to manage it responsibly and effectively to meet personal objectives and values, and tackle difficult questions like, 'How much is enough?' and how to think about advisors, family meetings, education, and charitable giving as part of one's legacy. And he does so in a remarkably practical way that is not theoretical and esoteric, like so many books are, but with actionable, down-to-earth, and easy-to-understand-and-implement ideas and guidance.

Ronald N. Quinn
Executive Vice President
Tenaska Energy, Inc.

While our organization helps facilitate complex gifts to charity, none of this happens until an individual is moved to action. **A Spectrum of Legacies** *does a masterful job of motivating individuals of affluence to action and to share some of their abundance with their communities. A wonderful read for tax advisors to share with their clients.*

Bryan Clontz, PhD, CFP®, CAP®
President
Charitable Solutions, LLC

Table of Contents

Dedication

I dedicate this book to my parents who used family meetings to pass on their personal values and to the many individuals who have embraced the responsibility of wealth by crafting legacies that benefit their families and communities.

I'm not an expert, just an observer.
I'm not uber wealthy, yet I have more than I need.
I am a father who is committed to his children and wants them
*   to be proud of themselves for being their best selves.*
I cannot change everything, but I can change some things.
I have been blessed in so many ways that I am filled with gratitude.
I accept the responsibility that comes with good fortune.
I will do what I can.

                                                    Mark Weber

Introduction

The price of greatness is responsibility.
WINSTON CHURCHILL

"I challenge you to make our community the most generous community per capita in the country!" Standing just 15 feet away, Warren Buffett seemed to be talking directly to me as he addressed that night's gathering of philanthropists. He continued, "Are you doing everything you can to make our community number one in giving?" His challenge rang in my ears that night and for the next couple of weeks when I decided to accept it.

Buffett issued that challenge over a decade ago at a United Way dinner and it continues to inspire me today in my work with families and in my role as a spouse and parent to five grown children. Ultimately, his challenge is the inspiration and goal for this book: I hope that what I share here will inspire you to teach your heirs to be stewards of their inheritance and for you to leave a legacy to your community.

I know that wealthy individuals rarely make significant charitable gifts without the advice and counsel of their professional advisors because I am one of those advisors. I have a law degree, a master's degree in financial services and several industry professional designations. Professionals in these disciplines tend to focus solely on the *tax aspects* of transferring assets.

Reaching professional advisors, I realized, was my key to meeting Mr. Buffett's challenge because we are typically present at the inflection point when individuals determine whether to make significant gifts to charity as part of their legacies.

Teaching professional advisors that there is so much more to leaving a legacy than simply avoiding taxes was my initial goal. The question was: how?

Since the mission of the Omaha Community Foundation includes "promoting philanthropy throughout the community," I proposed that it host the first study group of professional advisors. I believed that we could learn to ask our clients (individuals who were creating their estate plans) questions that would elicit their values, dreams and goals. If we actively listened to their responses, we could help individuals leave legacies that would benefit their families and communities and attach meaning to the financial assets they had worked a lifetime to accumulate. For the curriculum I chose the accredited Chartered Advisor in Philanthropy (CAP®) program from The American College of Financial Services.

I suggested that we invite a dozen local professional advisors to form the first study group. Simultaneously, members of the group would take the CAP® program's online classes and supplement those classes with 15 two-hour meetings. I would facilitate those meetings during which one speaker (or a panel) would make a presentation followed by candid discussion. The Foundation's leadership saw the potential and readily agreed.

Ten years later we have over 130 CAP® graduates in the Omaha area. Increasingly, estate planning professionals are able to help more individuals discover and create their legacies than ever before. In Omaha we are meeting Mr. Buffett's challenge one conversation at a time between philanthropically inclined individuals and advisors. Omaha CAP graduates estimate that their clients have made charitable gifts and bequests totaling $9 billion over the past ten years.

What is Legacy Planning?

When we think of our legacies (if we do!), we typically think in terms of traditional estate planning: passing *financial* assets to heirs at our deaths. Traditional estate planning does a good job of transferring financial assets tax efficiently, yet *it does little—if anything—to help us transfer our personal values to heirs.*

The legacy you create can be so much more than the transfer of financial assets. Your legacy can include:

· Teaching your children to become productive, contributing citizens and to manage wealth responsibly.

· Sharing your values about spending, saving, investing, and giving away wealth.

· Providing your children the tools they will need to get along with each other as adults, make difficult family decisions, contribute to their communities and pass on your values to their children.

Legacy planning then, is the work that you (and your advisors) do to distribute both your financial assets and values.

The process of intentionally passing both financial assets and your values surrounding those assets to your children can give your life meaning and build stronger families and communities.

What's the Problem?

From the time our children are toddlers and throughout their school years, we teach them our values: kindness, respecting others, honesty, playing by the rules, hard work, etc. We teach them very little about money and share little (or none) of our feelings about it. Only when parents die and children receive assets do most learn how much money they've inherited. And that manual that tells them how their parents want them to use the money? There isn't one.

Why, then, are we so surprised when our children prove incapable of managing large sums of money and fight with siblings about what they "think" their parents wanted?

What I Hope to Contribute

There are many excellent articles and books written on the various aspects of legacy planning and I've read many of them. In writing this book, I have synthesized what I've read with the best practices from three additional sources:
1. Thirty years of experience working with wealthy individuals,
2. Materials from the Chartered Advisor in Philanthropy® curriculum, and

The process of intentionally passing both financial assets and your values surrounding those assets to your children can give your life meaning and build stronger families and communities.

3. The life experiences and insights shared by some of the presenters to our CAP® Study Group.

From these sources, I offer the following insights:

· Signing your estate planning documents is not the end of the planning process. It is only one step on a spectrum of actions you can take to prepare children to inherit wealth responsibly.

· Determining the appropriate amount to leave children and teaching them how to use their inheritance responsibly are not tasks you can delegate. You must accept this responsibility and effectively communicate your wishes to your advisors.

· To live the final phase of your life with confidence that you will not outlive your resources and develop an effective legacy plan, you must work with your own personal board of advisors. I'm confident that you have the resources in your community to do both if you take the initiative to tell your advisors that you want more than a traditional estate plan.

· Legacy planning is an ongoing process rather than a one-time event. It takes initiative and effort on your part but the benefits to you, your children, your family as a whole and your community are enormous.

· There is no one way to leave a legacy. Once you determine what your legacy will be, there are steps you can take to determine where you wish to fall on the legacy spectrum.

Is Legacy Planning For You?

Whether you are an individual of modest means or great financial wealth, I encourage you to incorporate your values into your planning. Your role as your children's teacher doesn't end when your children finish school. If you have not communicated with your children about your values surrounding money, it is never too late to begin.

Leaving a legacy is a journey; one in which you set the terms. As you begin yours, I wish you the best. Enjoy it! The joy is in the journey.

What to Expect

In this book, I describe what several wealthy individuals have done to pass on their values—along with their money—to their children to inspire you to do the same. (Of course, I have altered the names and some of the facts to respect their confidentiality.) While these people possessed significant wealth, the techniques they used to accomplish their goals apply to individuals of more modest means.

Most of the examples in this book deal with wealthy, married couples around retirement age because that group describes my client base. Just as the techniques I recommend are effective regardless of wealth, they also apply whether a person is married or single, retirement age or younger.

The Legacy Spectrum

When I wrote *The Legacy Spectrum* five years ago, I intended it for two groups of readers: people of retirement age who were creating or updating their estate plans and their professional advisors. Since then, I've been overwhelmed by the number of notes and comments from individuals who have implemented some form of legacy planning and from advisors who have incorporated ideas from the book into their professional practices.

As you can see from the comments on the following pages, many individuals used the book to evaluate why and how much of an inheritance to leave their children. Most, however, described the transformational impact family meetings had on their families. Readers indicated that family relationships *had noticeably improved*, and they were confident *would continue to deepen with further meetings*. Other readers appreciated the guidance in creating a structure for writing their own personalized charitable giving plans. They reported that they found greater joy in giving when giving aligned with their values.

Here are some sample comments.

From clients and donors:

· *I now have the confidence I have enough to retire and a methodology to maintain that confidence.*

· *I articulated my core values and found it empowering.*

· *You gave me permission to decide if I want to (I do) leave an inheritance for my kids.*

· *Best method I have seen on how to determine on how much we should leave our children. Very helpful!*

· *We amended our estate plan to include a significant charitable bequest.*

· *We wrote our own personal giving plan and started giving more. It is far more rewarding giving as a couple in alignment with our giving plan.*

· *We started holding family meetings with our adult children and have encouraged several of our friends to do the same. It's fun!*

· *My husband and I have each written letters to our children and put them with our estate plan. It was an emotional experience, and we're glad we did it.*

· *We now invite our children to make limited distributions from our donor advised fund. It has been rewarding and insightful. We are learning more about our children. We love it.*

· *We formed our own Personal Board of Advisors and look forward to our advisors collaborating on keeping us on track in our later years.*

From adult children:

· *I gave a copy to my father for his birthday to prod him to start his own planning.*

· *We gave a book to my parents with the chapter on family meetings highlighted. We are hopeful they will see the wisdom of starting our own family meetings.*

· *My parents are so concerned about leaving a big inheritance to us kids, but I don't need it. I gave them the book and pointed out the parts about giving to the community.*

· *I shared with my 80-year-old mom the idea in the book about having her retirement account pass to a donor advised fund for me rather than an inheritance. Great idea!*

From professional advisors:

· *I give the book to clients with a note to focus on the chapter on personal values and ask them to write their own values down before they meet with me again.*

· *I give the book to clients that I think could really benefit from family meetings.*

· *My client has never introduced me to his other advisors. I gave him a copy of the book with a note on the chapter on working collaboratively as an advisor team.*

· *My favorite widow client is struggling on who to give her money to when she dies. I gave her your book with a note on the story of the widower who learned to be charitable.*

· *I gave a copy of your book to each of the board members of a closely held company on which I am corporate legal counsel. They all seem to struggle with how much to leave their children. The responsibility of wealth part was right on point!*

From nonprofit organizations:

· *We send [the book] to select donors to introduce the idea of transitioning from "default" planning to "legacy" planning.*

· *I have sent your book to several of our top annual givers to prompt them to leave us an "ultimate" gift in their will.*

· *I have sent the book to families I think could benefit by giving as a family to teach their children the joy of giving. I point out the stories of families giving together.*

· *We gave a copy to each member of our board of advisors as a "thank you."*

· *To kick off our Planned Giving Campaign, we sent a copy of your book to each donor before we scheduled our one-on-one meetings with them.*

· *We recently established a Professional Advisor Council and gave each advisor a copy of your book (with a bookmark on the page on advisor collaboration).*

In response to this confirmation that the ideas in my first book do make a difference in families and communities, I wrote this one to include:

· More stories.

· New ideas for holding successful family meetings.

· Guidelines to help you identify your core personal values.

· Tips to make your charitable giving more inspirational.

· More sample letters for you to incorporate into your own legacy plan.

I hope you find this book to be a valuable resource that you can use, and share. If you are an advisor, I hope this book will help you offer broader, more meaningful counsel to your clients. If you are not an advisor, I hope it inspires you to accept and embrace the responsibility that comes with wealth and draws your family closer through giving to others. No matter who you are I challenge you to think beyond passing simply monetary wealth.

Most of all, I hope you will apply what you learn to make a positive impact on the people and organizations most important to you.

CHAPTER 1

Wealth In America

Seek not greater wealth, but simpler pleasure;
not higher fortune, but deeper felicity.
MAHATMA GANDHI

Ours is the wealthiest nation in the world, and we are in the middle of the greatest intergenerational transfer of wealth in our history. Individuals in the "second half" of their lives are driving this transfer, and many of them want to transfer their values along with their money to the next generation.

The Problem

Traditional estate planning is designed to pass our wealth in as tax-efficient manner as possible and it does a great job doing so. Traditional estate planning is not, however, designed to help us pass our values to our heirs or prepare them to manage significant financial resources. It falls far short of the goals more and more of us want to accomplish for ourselves and for our heirs as we pass down our assets:

· Tax minimization
· Values education
· Financial management skills

In the first half of life, we raise our children and work to instill in them—typically by example—our values. Once they finish their formal education and leave our homes, we assume our job as parents is complete. Rarely do parents give children practical financial education, much less preparation to inherit financial assets. The first time most heirs learn about their parents' finances is when they read their deceased parents' wills in an attorney's office.

Given our failure to articulate our values, educate our children about financial matters and link the two, can we really be surprised when children are unprepared to handle a large inheritance and that families fracture in fights over parents' money?

The Solution

There is an alternative to passing assets in a way that fails to prepare children to manage them and prevent families from breaking apart because there's no "glue" holding them together after parents die. That alternative and supplement to traditional estate planning is legacy planning.

The legacy planning that we'll discuss in this book gives parents a forum to 1) clearly articulate their values and 2) prepare their children to manage wealth responsibly.

There is an alternative to passing assets in a way that fails to prepare children to manage them and prevent families from breaking apart because there's no "glue" holding them together…

Legacy Planning Raises The Bar.

I will share the personal stories of some families who have used legacy planning to supplement their traditional estate plans. Their legacy plans pass on their values as well as their wealth. They have done far more than sign legal documents.

Legacy plans:

1. Give you the confidence to live your remaining years free of financial fear.

2. Enrich your relationship with your children.

3. Teach your children to use their inheritance in accordance with your values.

4. Nurture your soul by giving back to your community and

inspiring your children to do the same.

5. Maximize the value of your professional advisors.

Legacy planning gives parents an effective way to prepare heirs to receive wealth and intentionally transfer their values, and provides a platform for inter- and intra-generational interaction.

Legacy planning gives parents an effective way to prepare heirs to receive wealth and intentionally transfer their values…

WHO'S GOT THE MONEY?

Research suggests that as much as $70 trillion will change hands in the coming decades as the older generations die and pass wealth to their children.[1] Before I ask a few questions that will give you context for the decisions you will make about your own wealth, it is helpful to understand how generations are divided and which ones currently hold the wealth.

· If you were born before 1945, you are part of the "World War II," or "Silent Generation."

· If you were born between 1946 and 1964, you are a "Baby Boomer."

· If you were born between 1965 and 1980, you are a "GenXer."

· If you were born between 1980 and the early 1990s, you are a "Millennial."

· The "Next Gen" often refers to the combined generations of "GenXers" and "Millennials."

Question 1: Who do you think owns most of the wealth in the United States?

Despite the near daily publicity surrounding the mind-boggling

---

1 *https://info.cerulli.com/HNW-Transfer-of-Wealth-Cerulli.html*

wealth being amassed by young Silicon Valley tech billionaires from Amazon, Tesla, Google and Facebook, baby boomers and their parents control as much as three-quarters of the wealth in America![2] That's why so many of the comments in this book are addressed to the "seventy-five percent."

Question 2: How important is it to you to leave an inheritance?

My purpose in asking this question is not to judge whether leaving money to children is a good or bad thing. Rather, it is to prompt you to consider *why* (like most of us) you desire to leave an inheritance *before* you determine how much you will pass.

Have you and your spouse ever had a frank conversation about why each of you wishes to leave money to your children? If you have, have you discussed how much money you wish to leave them? Are you both in agreement? Or does one of you want to leave this world having spent your last dollar, while the other feels an obligation to leave your children holding a big pile of cash?

The key is to openly discuss these questions with each other, come to a consensus and clearly communicate your wishes to your professional advisors.

Question 3: If you decide to leave an inheritance, how confident are you that your heirs can handle the assets you leave?

In my experience, it is common for parents to wonder whether a large inheritance would have a detrimental effect on their children. This is particularly true for grandparents who contemplate leaving money to grandchildren. There is one group of parents, however, that often does not share this concern: parents who have worked, usually for years, with their children in family businesses. First, these parents have had the opportunity to mentor their children and watch their children make increasingly important business/financial decisions. Second, the assets these parents are passing are in the form of inventory,

---

[2] *For more information about generational wealth, see the* Distribution of Household Wealth in the U.S. since 1989 *provided by the Board of Governors of the Federal Reserve System.*
https://www.federalreserve.gov/releases/z1/dataviz/dfa/distribute/table/#quarter:119;series:Net%20 worth;demographic:generation;popluation:all;units:levels

equipment, real estate and goodwill rather than cash. Parents who own family businesses generally express far more confidence in their children's ability to handle an inheritance than do parents who contemplate passing cash or other liquid assets.

Newspapers and online news sources are full of stories about sudden wealth and beneficiaries who fell prey to predators, financial hucksters and exotic investment schemes. Many were broke in just a few years. Others, addicted to easy money, never achieved their true potential.

...it is common for parents to wonder whether a large inheritance would have a detrimental effect on their children.

Still, many parents who know these stories leave their children significant inheritances. They do so because they want their children to sidestep some of the hardships they experienced on their paths to financial success. They believe that the best way to smooth their child's path in life is cash: multiple and large gifts of cash. In this belief, they remind me of the story of the man and the cocoon.

One day a man found a butterfly cocoon with a small opening. He sat and watched for hours as the tiny butterfly struggled to force its body through that little hole. Then the butterfly stopped making progress. It appeared as if it could go no further.

So, the man decided to help the butterfly. With a pair of scissors, he snipped off the remaining bit of the cocoon. The butterfly then emerged easily, but it had a swollen body and small, shriveled wings. The man continued to watch the butterfly because he expected that, at any moment, its wings would enlarge and expand, and its swollen body would contract.

Neither happened! In fact, the butterfly spent the rest of its short life crawling on the ground with a swollen body and shriveled wings. It never was able to fly.

What the man, in his kindness and haste, did not understand was that the restricting cocoon forced the butterfly to struggle to get through the tiny opening. This design was God's way of forcing the fluid from the body of the butterfly into its wings so that the butterfly could fly once it freed itself from the cocoon.

Sometimes struggles are exactly what we need to be successful in our lives. If God allowed us to go through our lives without any obstacles, we would never reach our full potential. We would not be as strong as we are after overcoming challenges. Without struggle we cannot fly!

The desire to protect our children is a good thing when they are young. As they age, however, if we become helicopter parents and don't give children the tools to overcome challenges and "rescue" themselves, we rob them of the possibility of becoming independent, confident adults.

Our current system of estate planning does nothing to help parents teach children to manage the wealth they will receive. Nor does it adequately tackle the other issue that the owners of our country's wealth are most concerned about: Passing on values and life lessons.

Question 4: What do you feel is the most important inheritance you can pass to your heirs?

Surprisingly, or perhaps not, wealthy families tell researchers that money is one of the least important "assets" they plan to leave to their children. Topping the list are values and life lessons.

To understand why our current estate planning process is simply not conducive to passing parental values and lessons to children, nor equipping children to responsibly manage large financial inheritances, let's look at how estate planning is usually approached.

HOW MOST OF US APPROACH ESTATE PLANNING

Virtually no one looks forward with excitement to creating an estate plan. While we want to make certain that we provide for those we love, there is little appeal in facing our own mortality and giving away assets we've spent a lifetime accumulating. A feeling of obligation to our children and duty to "plan" for our deaths motivate most of us to call an estate planning attorney.

Prior to our first meeting with an attorney, spouses typically spend precious little time answering the questions I've asked here, much less discussing, clarifying, and prioritizing their goals. Pre-meeting conversations usually begin and end with, "I want to make certain you are financially secure. After you die, the kids can have whatever money is left. Do you want to meet me at the attorney's office or will we go together?"

We give no thought to:

· The values we, as parents, want to pass on to our children,

· How we want our children to use the money we leave,

· Whether an inheritance will have a constructive or destructive effect on our children, and

· How we might use a portion of our wealth to express our gratitude for all that we've received.

Certainly, we don't commit much time, if any, to considering how the estate plan we are about to create could bring our families closer together and provide us an opportunity to educate our children.

We leave estate planning attorneys to make their own assumptions because we provide no information about:

· Why we wish to pass an inheritance to our children,

· How we want our children to use that inheritance,

· What values we want to guide our planning, or

· Whether we would like to leave a charitable bequest to the nonprofits we care about.

It's time to take the initiative!

In the chapters that follow, you will learn how to supplement your estate plan with a legacy plan that passes your financial assets *and values* to your heirs. That plan will also:

· **Bring** you closer as a family.

· **Communicate** your values about money to your children.

· **Give** your children the tools they need to use the assets you leave wisely.

· **Attach** meaning to your financial assets as you use them to give back to your community.

A legacy plan requires you to take the initiative. You must set the course and tell your advisors that you want their help. Unless your advisors understand legacy planning, you may need to introduce them to the concept.

Setting Your Course

I've created the worksheets in this book to help you and your spouse create the outline for your own legacy plan. (See Chapter 8 or visit *SpectrumOfLegacies.com* to download them.) Worksheets will spark conversation and help you define the type and size of inheritance most appropriate for your family. Only when you and your spouse have come to an agreement and gained clarity about your goals can you articulate them to your advisors. Armed with that information, your advisors can pick up the ball and create a plan, a legacy plan, that carries out your wishes.

You can do this. I know because most of the people whose stories appear in this book all started where you are: They all had worked with experienced, highly skilled estate planning attorneys to pass financial assets to their children, but they wanted to pass their values as well. In the end, the estate plans that they created evolved into legacy plans because they worked with their advisors and accomplished far more than just a tax-advantaged distribution of assets.

The Stakes Are High and The Rewards Are Great.

There is no room in traditional estate planning for preparing children to responsibly handle a large inheritance. Nor do traditional estate plans do a good job of passing on our values and life lessons to our children.

If we continue to do estate planning in the "traditional" way, assets will continue to flow to heirs unprepared to manage them. Our values will disappear with us. We will just have to hope that the financial assets we leave to our children will enhance their lives rather than destroy them. We can do better that this!

In the midst of this historic transfer of wealth, it is up to each of us to do what we can to ensure that our heirs manage our share of that wealth wisely after we die. By incorporating legacy planning into our estate plans, we take the initiative to positively impact our families and communities.

CHAPTER 2

How To Know When You Have Enough

If you look at what you have in life, you'll always have more.
If you look at what you don't have in life, you'll never have enough.
OPRAH WINFREY

Before we can do any meaningful estate planning, it is essential to be confident that we will have financial security in our later years. During our lifetime, we will not make significant lifetime gifts to our children, much less our communities, if we fret over whether we will have enough for ourselves.

Few people know how to achieve that confidence, erroneously thinking that greater net worth automatically assures financial security. Instead, financial security comes from building your own Roadmap to Confidence—a roadmap to take you from where you are today to being confident that you have enough. This chapter describes the five steps to building your Roadmap and outlines how you can maintain that confidence for the rest of your life.

DETERMINING HOW MUCH IS ENOUGH FOR YOU

We spend our working careers, often 40 to 50 years or more, generating enough money to support ourselves during both our working and retirement years. Once income from our labor ceases and we are dependent on investment earnings, it can be disconcerting.

It is quite common and natural to be concerned about any or all of the following stressors:

· **What if** my spouse suddenly dies?

· **What if** we encounter a medical emergency?

· **What if** one (or both) of us gets Alzheimer's?

· **What if** one (or both) of us has to go into a nursing home?

· **What if** one of our children gets divorced and/or needs significant financial help?

· *What if…?*

Thinking about how any or all of these events can affect your life is natural and a necessary first step toward confidence in having enough.

What Is Your Retirement Number?

An insurance company took a clever approach to calculating "enough" during one's retirement years in one of its television commercials. An actor posits the question, "What is your number?" and the camera follows people carrying placards of their "number," (e.g., $3,643,201 or $5,127,989, etc.) while engaged in daily activities. It is a clever and effective way to make the point that we should calculate how much money we must accumulate to generate enough income during retirement to replace the incomes we enjoyed during our working years.

The number or dollar amount that gives you confidence in your ability to live comfortably throughout your retirement years is the result of a multi-faceted process that takes some time and requires input from financial professionals.

In reality, however, this equation is more complex than punching some numbers into a calculator. The number or dollar amount that gives you confidence in your ability to live comfortably throughout your retirement years is the result of a multi-faceted process that takes some time and requires input from financial professionals.

Not only is the calculation more complicated than advertised, the amount of funds we need to live comfortably during retirement is not static. We've been led to believe that if we build a big enough pile of chips at retirement, we will live a worry-free life, sipping cold drinks on a warm beach in paradise!

Unfortunately, retirement doesn't work that way. Retirement is not a point in time, but another phase of our lives. The person we are now is not the person we will be then. For example, if we are worriers now, we will worry then.

The stressors mentioned in this chapter never really go away. In fact, anxiety can grow as we age. When that happens, many people are never confident that they have enough.

Building Your Roadmap To Confidence, Step By Step

The very first step in answering the question "How much is enough to assure my financial security?" is to capture a clear picture of the amount of cash you currently spend. All subsequent steps rest on that foundation.

Step One: Establish A Current Budget.

I am constantly amazed by how few people develop and maintain a household budget. By "budget," I do not mean recording every dollar you spend on an electronic spreadsheet, although doing so is excellent discipline when you first establish a household!

I'm talking about having a clear understanding of how much spendable income you need to maintain your current lifestyle. You can calculate this income amount yourself by reviewing your checkbook and credit card bills for the last couple of years. Alternatively, you can hire your accounting firm to do it for you. Ask your advisors to review your calculations so they identify items you may have forgotten and can help you build in a cushion for unforeseen emergencies. Whether you collect the data yourself or have your accountant do so, you need to be comfortable with the ultimate result.

Step Two: Project Future Income and Expenses.

Your current budget is the foundation for estimating the amount of cash you'll need during your retirement years. To calculate that number, you and your advisors will answer a multitude of questions:

· What income will you receive (from, for example, Social Security, pension, 401(k), deferred compensation, interest, and dividends)?

· Will certain expenses decrease? These might include 401(k) contributions, private medical insurance, disability insurance premiums and payroll deductions.

· Will certain expenses increase? These might include travel or expenses associated with a second home.

· What inflation rate is reasonable to expect?

· What is a reasonable rate of return to expect?

· What will your income taxes likely be?

· What is the realistic life expectancy for you and your spouse?

· When should you start to take Social Security benefits?

· Which assets should you spend first?

Skilled retirement planners use sophisticated software programs to help you test various answers to these questions. In my experience these specialists can be hugely helpful in the retirement planning process. They have helped dozens of people just like you and understand what you are going through.

Step Three: Stress Test Your Future Budget.

It is completely natural to have lingering doubts about a well-thought-out budget. I'll bet you can think of a million things that might torpedo yours. For example, how will your budget be affected if the stock market takes a nosedive, you run up major medical bills, or your children need financial help?

The simple act of making a written list of your concerns can be cathartic and expose unconscious, unnamed fears to the light of day. From this perspective you can examine, discuss, and address them.

Your list of questions and concerns will change over time as you and the world around you change. What is important is to continually acknowledge any fears to ourselves and to our advisors.

Step Four: Factor In Your Emotions.

In addition to the quantitative information necessary to create your Roadmap To Confidence, there are qualitative issues (psychological and emotional factors) to consider. As we move further away from our income-generating years, it is natural to feel more financially vulnerable. Similarly, as our bodies age, we find ourselves increasingly dependent on others. We can become fearful when we feel vulnerable.

As we move further away from our income-generating years, it is natural to feel more financially vulnerable.

A certain amount of fear is healthy: it makes us evaluate the accuracy and breadth of our calculation of actual and projected expenses as well as our stress testing. Comprehensive calculations can yield confidence for some but for most of us there's also an emotional component to our "enough number."

To illustrate that having enough is not solely an objective, mathematical calculation, I share a few stories.

The Paralysis Of Fear

A client once asked me to help his father ("George") update his estate plan. George was about 85 years old and had sold a very successful, third-generation business ten years before. Almost his entire nest egg of $50,000,000 was in bank accounts and the stock market. George and his wife ("Mildred") lived frugally and spent between $100,000 to $120,000 on living expenses per year. George reinvested virtually all of his investment earnings.

George and Mildred had simple wills leaving their assets to each other and whatever was left, equally to their children. George's primary estate planning goals were: 1) financial security for Mildred and himself, and 2) leave as much as they *could to their adult children. I pointed out to George that since his investment earnings alone exceeded $1,000,000 annually, he had more money than he could ever spend.*

I suggested that to meet his goals, George and Mildred begin making lifetime gifts to their children and grandchildren to reduce the size of their taxable estate and shift future appreciation of assets to their children.

George rejected my suggestions. He explained that he had lived through the Great Depression, saw the stock market crash, banks fail, and his parents lose everything. Despite being a multimillionaire, George never felt he had "enough."

This fear froze both George and Mildred into inaction. As a result of their unwillingness to make transfers to their children during their lifetimes, the estate paid nearly $20,000,000 in estate taxes. Had George and Mildred been able to overcome their fears of not having "enough," much of the $20,000,000 could have been directed to their children, grandchildren and/or the charities they cared about.

By any objective measure, George and Mildred had more than enough money to retire free of worry. Yet they feared the worst until the very end.

I am not making light of George and Mildred's fears. They were so paralyzed by fear that no amount of money, no matter how carefully calculated, could be enough. In George and Mildred's case, that fear arose from watching their parents struggle.

· In 1933, the unemployment rate was 25 percent.

· In 1933, on average 1,000 home mortgages were foreclosed every day.[3]

· Average family income fell (on average) 40% between 1929 and 1933.

---

[3] *Federal Home Loan Bank Board, 1937, p. 4, as quoted in Changing the Rules: State Mortgage Foreclosure Moratoria During the Great Depression, David C. Wheelock, Federal Reserve Bank of St. Louis, Review, November/December 2008, 90(6), pp. 569-583. https://files.stlouisfed.org/files/htdocs/publications/review/08/11/Wheelock.pdf*

While we cannot control much of what happens to us throughout our lives, we can control how we react to each challenge thrown our way. The next story illustrates how a person (about the same age as George and Mildred) can have a similar life experience, a much smaller net worth, and yet be confident that they have enough.

Confidence Creates A Legacy.
"Steven" was an 85-year-old widower who had two married children. He and his wife had sold their dry-cleaning business several years before she died, had invested the proceeds wisely and lived modestly. After his wife's death, Steven focused his attention on his collections of coins and international travel with the Roads Scholar educational tours.

Steven's net worth was over $7,000,000 and he spent approximately $300,000 each year. His estate plan provided a generous inheritance to his two children as well as a significant charitable bequest to Steven's alma mater.

He worked with his advisors to review his financial situation and took great comfort in knowing that he was spending only income and not chipping away at principal. In fact, his estate was growing. He realized that if he ever decided to spend more, he could spend down some principal and still have plenty to pass on to his children. In fact, his advisors reassured Steven that he had plenty of money and could feel free to take more trips or make lifetime gifts to his children and alma mater.

The stories of Steven and George (and Mildred) illustrate how two eighty-five-year-olds can feel completely differently about their

While we cannot control much of what happens to us throughout our lives, we can control how we react to each challenge thrown our way.

financial security. Steven felt confident in his financial security while George and Mildred lived in fear of running out of money.

While we can attribute some of George and Mildred's fear to childhood experience, I believe that a good portion can be attributed to a lack of trust in others, particularly an unwillingness to engage with professional advisors and solicit their input regarding financial and retirement planning. George and Mildred were victims of their own fears.

Is Your Fear Justified?

If you identify with George and Mildred, you are far from alone. Surveys indicate that running out of money is a common concern, even among the affluent. Rather than ignore or make light of that fear, I suggest that you do some introspection and confront it before engaging advisors.

Too often, spouses consult only each other. If one is a doomsdayer, that spouse can suck the other one down so they both become frightened of the future. They fuel each other's fears. Talking about the possibility of running out of money in a candid, objective manner with a close friend, sibling or adult child can halt this spiral and put fears into perspective. Often, with input from a trusted outsider, we can see the world more clearly. Once we identify and list realistic fears, we can bring that list to our professional advisors.

Advisors can help you realistically confront your fears only if they know they exist.

Concern about the future is completely normal, and it is important to acknowledge and express those concerns or fears to advisors—as both George and Steven did. Too often, we don't mention our fears to our advisors for reasons that range from embarrassment to a desire to avoid the fees that accompany spending time with an advisor.

Believe it or not, your advisors are likely as concerned about charging you fees as you are with incurring them. For this reason, most are reluctant to raise emotionally difficult topics—topics that take time to discuss.

For these reasons, it is important to your peace of mind that you bring up any fears you have, and give your advisors the opportunity to really listen, understand, and help you work through them. Only through that process can you hope to gain confidence in your future financial security.

Step Five: Let Your Advisors Help You.

I have come to believe that most of us will never feel fully financially secure if we try to achieve that confidence alone. Despite how irrational our fears may be, they are very real to us. Fears resurface and the amount we need to feel secure always seems to be slightly more than we have!

...most of us will never feel fully financially secure if we try to achieve that confidence alone.

If we share with them our fears, advisors can inject reason by turning problems into workable solutions. When they address our concerns on a regular and ongoing basis, they can tamp them down.

Confidence comes from experiencing success on a consistent basis.

Without regular reinforcement from professional advisors we trust, our fears can take hold and take control of our decisions. Experienced advisors can shine a light on those fears as they arise, answer our "What If?" questions and even pose questions we haven't thought of.

In doing so, they not only help us put our fears in perspective, but they also help us to recognize the wisdom of the plans we've put in place for our financial security. (In the coming pages we'll talk about how to build, and use, a team of advisors that can answer your questions and provide the reinforcement you need.)

Confidence comes from experiencing success on a consistent basis.

Conclusion

There is more to feeling confident in our financial security during our retirement years than building substantial net worth. We must acknowledge that fear is a natural emotion, confront it, and constantly address it. The five steps in Building Your Roadmap To Confidence are:

1. Establish a current budget.

2. Project future income and expenses.

3. Stress test your future budget.

4. Factor in your emotions

5. Let your advisors help you.

Taking these steps and meeting regularly with your professional advisors is the best way to build and retain confidence that you have enough to be financially secure during your retirement years

Confidence that you have enough enables you to live the last phase of your life not in a state of scarcity but of abundance. Confidence is also the critical prerequisite to tackling the questions:

1. How much should I leave my children?

2. What will my legacy be?

CHAPTER 3

Values-Driven Planning

*It's not hard to make decisions when you
know what your values are.*
ROY DISNEY

Our personal values help us formulate how we interact with the world around us. Values are something we hold in esteem and aspire to. In a sense, they are "guardrails" for our beliefs and behavior. We feel best about ourselves when our actions are in alignment with our values. A partial list of values follows. You may wish to add your own.

Values

Abundance	Ethics	Independence
Acceptance	Excellence	Integrity
Accountability	Fairness	Intelligence
Achievement	Faith	Involvement
Appreciation	Financial	Justice
Commitment	Independence	Kindness
Compassion	Fitness	Knowledge
Competence	Forgiveness	Leadership
Contribution	Frugality	Love
Courage	Generosity	Loyalty
Dependability	Gratitude	Modesty
Determination	Health	Patience
Discipline	Honesty	Perseverance
Education	Honor	Pride
Empathy	Humility	Productivity

Recognition	Sacrifice	Sharing
Respect	Self-control	Success
Responsibility	Self-reliance	Trustworthiness
Restraint	Self-respect	Wisdom

You may find a number of values with which you identify. (A wonderful, easy-to-read book to help you identify your core values so you can live by them is *Riveted: 44 Values That Change the World* by David R. York and Andrew L. Howell.) I encourage you to narrow the list to your top three to four core values, then write a phrase or sentence that best describes the value from your unique perspective.

For example:

Courage: Mental or moral strength to persevere in the face of great resistance or difficulty

Accountability: Holding oneself responsible for her own actions

Determination: Fixed intention and unrelenting commitment to achieve a desired result

Why is narrowing your list and assigning your definition important? You might be surprised to learn that in survey after survey, the single most important thing high-net worth individuals want to pass to their children, is not money, but personal values!

Money has little intrinsic value, but it may be used for great good or great harm. Our personal values, however, do have intrinsic worth; they provide us a sense of contentment, of personal meaning, and come from a lifetime of experience. It is this sense of self-fulfillment and wisdom gained from our experiences that so many wish to pass on to heirs.

Unfortunately, personal values have little place in the traditional estate planning process. Individuals are asked questions that revolve around data like names, dates of birth, addresses, marital status, children, state of residence, etc. This data, combined with a current personal financial statement, is enough information to prepare most estate planning documents. The process, to a growing extent, has become "mechanical." Whether in-person or online, there are no questions related to one's personal values. This book hopes to change that process. The very foundation of legacy (or values-driven) planning is your personal values. The following story may make the distinction between traditional and values-driven planning clear.

A Mother's Values-Driven Plan

"Ruth" and "James," both just 22, drove north 800 miles to begin their married life together. Despite strenuous objections from their parents, Ruth and James were on an adventure and determined to make their own way. James accepted a management-trainee position with the railroad and Ruth as a secretary. Within a few years, the couple had two small boys, and they decided that Ruth would stay home with their growing family.

Our personal values, however, do have intrinsic worth; they provide us a sense of contentment, of personal meaning, and come from a lifetime of experience.

When their boys were just five and seven, James was killed in a freak work accident. Ruth and James' parents implored her to come back home where they could help her raise her sons. But Ruth was adamant. She'd made a new home and was determined to continue the dream she and James had agreed upon to make a better life for themselves.

Ruth quickly determined that the life insurance proceeds would not be sufficient to raise and educate her boys, so she would start her own business. Subleasing a small space in the back of a beauty salon, Ruth began a childcare business. Despite the first painfully slow couple of years, Ruth refused to give up her dream of self-sufficiency. Over the next 25 years Ruth built her business which, at three locations, was the largest non-

franchised daycare center in her adopted hometown. Her two boys, now 31 and 33, were both college graduates and gainfully employed. Both boys respected their mother and remained close to her.

Ruth and James had wills prepared when the boys were babies. Now that Ruth was 58 and had a grandchild on the way, she determined that it was time to update her estate plan. Before she scheduled an appointment with an attorney, she first met with her long-time financial planner, Tonya, to update her personal financial statement. Tonya had recently pursued training in values-driven planning, so asked Ruth to name her top three core values. After some reflection, Ruth identified the following values:

Courage. *She and James had the courage to leave home and move to a city where they knew no one to start a life of their own.*

Accountability. *Ruth knew that only she was responsible for her success and happiness in the world.*

Determination. *Despite the many hardships, Ruth had risked everything to make her business successful enough to support her family and educate her boys.*

Tonya and Ruth concurred that upon Ruth's death, the boys would have no interest in the business and would no doubt sell it. If they did so, each son would probably receive between $1,000,000 to $1,500,000 in cash. These funds would enable them to work just part-time or significantly enhance their lifestyle if they chose. Ruth had never thought about what her sons might do with an inheritance. Ruth did not want to deprive her sons of the tremendous sense of pride and self-satisfaction that she had gained from the hard work and perseverance it had taken to create a successful business. Since they were small, Ruth had drilled into her sons the need to earn their own way because in life there are no free handouts.

Tonya suggested that Ruth meet with an attorney who understood the merit of incorporating personal values in one's estate plan. In addition, Tonya convinced Ruth to begin to hold family meetings with her boys to pass on her values and teach them to be financially responsible with the inheritance they would eventually receive.

The estate plan that Ruth and her attorney drew up included:

· *A very personal letter that Ruth wrote to each of her sons describing her values; why she chose to leave them an inheritance; how much it would be; what she expected them to do with it; how they should be stewards of the money; and why she was contributing money to help young women start their own businesses.*

· *A fund to help pay college tuition for her future grandchildren.*

· *A trust designed to teach her sons how to manage money and protect it from creditors.*

Had Ruth not consulted Tonya, she almost certainly would have ended up with a traditional ("default") estate plan that distributed outright to her sons all the money she had accumulated over her lifetime—something she NEVER would have done when she was alive! With a values-driven plan, however, Ruth felt confident that upon her death her sons would fulfill her wishes and carry on her personal values.

In the following chapters I will build on this theme of constructing your estate plan and your legacy around your personal values.

CHAPTER 4

Deciding How Much
To Leave Children

*Americans are like a rich father who wishes he knew how
to give his sons the hardships that made him rich.*
ROBERT FROST

I n Chapter 2, we learned how to determine how much is enough
to sustain us during our retirement years and how to maintain
confidence that we'll have enough over time. Now we can build
on that foundation and have a meaningful discussion of the often-
asked question, "How much should I leave my children?"

"DEFAULT" ESTATE PLANNING

Traditional (or "default") estate planning presupposes that we wish
to leave our assets to our children. Even if you die without a will, state
intestacy laws distribute a portion of your assets to your children.

For these reasons, I refer to traditional estate planning as "default"
estate planning. Default planning takes for granted that you wish to
leave all (or nearly all) of your assets to your children. I'd ask you to
take a step back and ask why? Specifically, why do we want to leave
assets to our children?

Studies show that parents leave money to their children for a variety
of reasons including:
- **Express** feelings of affection

- **Preserve** family wealth

- **Carry on** a family tradition

· **Fulfill** a moral obligation

· **Minimize** taxes

· **Compensate** for past wrongs

In default estate planning, planners virtually never ask their clients, "Why do you want to leave assets to your children?" In fact, individuals planning their estates rarely ask themselves that question. It is simply the default assumption that if we have wealth, we want to pass it to our children. Understand that you have a choice. Examine, acknowledge, and communicate the reasons for your choice to your advisors. This will help them customize a plan for you that achieves your specific goals.

When we were young and starting out, passing the little that we had to our children made perfect sense. Worrying that they would receive "too much" was the last thing on our minds!

Fast forward to today: We have accumulated more wealth than we thought possible when we first started out. Today, there will be enough left over upon our deaths to have a very dramatic effect on the children who will receive it. Yet, the basic template of our estate plans has changed little. While our plans are more complex, our default position remains the same: ultimately transfer all our assets to our children.

As a result of the enormous wealth created in our country over the past 50 years, many wealth-holders are questioning this default position. When they ask themselves, "Why do I want to leave assets to my children?" they'll answer, "Because I love them." Many have come to believe, however, that too much money can be detrimental to their children's personal growth and happiness. The most prominent examples include Warren Buffett, Bill Gates and Mark Zuckerberg. Throughout this book you will find other wealth-holders who have come to similar conclusions.

The Great Irony Of Default Estate Planning

One of the great ironies of default estate planning is that it passes our money to our heirs in a manner completely contradictory to how we amassed it! Think about it. How do most people accumulate their wealth? Typically, they acquire education and/or specialized training in a particular area. Next, they take great risk—frequently failing multiple times before succeeding. Great self-sacrifice and self-discipline to live within one's means is demanded—at least in the early years.

Americans love the "rags-to-riches" stories of our greatest entrepreneurs. We don't begrudge those who overcome human tragedy and the obstacles life throws in their way. Rather, we revere these successful entrepreneurs. Most of them agree that hard work and sacrifice forged their character and gave them a great sense of satisfaction. Without the struggle, they would not be the people they are today.

But what do these same successful individuals do when they create their estate plans? They do—upon death—something they would NEVER do

One of the great ironies of default estate planning is that it passes our money to our heirs in a manner completely contradictory to how we amassed it!

during their lifetimes! They shower their children with the money it took a lifetime for them to accumulate; no training, no direction and none of the sense of personal accomplishment that accompanies earning it! As a result, many heirs spend inherited assets far more freely than they would money they themselves earned. I believe that this lack of training, direction and sense of personal accomplishment is the primary reason that heirs spend the average inheritance in just a few years!

The purpose of this chapter is to get you to challenge the default assumption. I want you to turn your focus inward and honestly answer the question, "Why do I want to leave money to my children?" To help you make that decision, I suggest that you use the Worksheet in Chapter 8, *Why We Choose To Leave Money To Our Children*. Once you, and your spouse each answer that question and, assuming you decide to leave your children something, it will be easier for you to grapple with the "how much?" question.

If you decide to leave a very large sum of money to your children, we will discuss how you might prepare them to handle it responsibly in Chapter 5. Alternatively, if you elect to leave them only enough to accomplish your goals for them and leave the rest to a cause or organization in your community, we'll discuss those issues in Chapter 6.

Regardless of which option you choose, the key is to pause and be thoughtful about the amount of money you wish to leave your children. Be deliberate and purposeful. Don't settle for default planning.

I believe that this lack of training, direction and sense of personal accomplishment is the primary reason that heirs spend the average inheritance in just a few years!

QUANTIFYING ENOUGH: A PROCESS TO DETERMINE HOW MUCH TO LEAVE CHILDREN

I have been asked, "How much money should I leave my children?" innumerable times. Typically, the question comes up in the context of an estate planning engagement, but not always. I've also been asked when playing golf, sitting at a college basketball game and a few times at cocktail parties. The question often comes from people I haven't worked with and whose children I don't even know! Do these folks assume that there is a "norm" that only professional advisors know about? Do they really expect me to say, "Oh, about $1,000,000" or "Two million dollars should be plenty!"?

Despite the naiveté of the question, it tells me that the person asking:

· **Cares** about their children.
· **Assumes** (since it is inherent in the question) that leaving too much money to children may be detrimental to their happiness and wellbeing.

They are right in assuming that leaving children "too much" money may do more harm than good. But soliciting the opinion of a professional advisor at a cocktail party is not the best way to determine the answer. The amount of money you decide to leave to your children is highly personal and depends on a number of factors related to your situation and to your children. It takes meaningful thought and dialogue between parents to arrive at an appropriate amount. Furthermore, this figure may change over time based on your net worth, competing interests for your money, your relationship with your children and their own financial situations.

I've created a process or exercise that you can use to answer the "How much do I leave to my kids?" question. I assure you that this process yields results that suit you and your family far better than those you'll receive via cocktail party opinions! Still this process is not prescriptive: there is no one right answer. For example, you know that each child is a product of his or her environment and life experience. An inheritance of $1,000,000 might be an incredible windfall for a child from one family, raised in one environment, but barely enough to cover a couple of years of expenses for another child raised in a very different environment. The process I propose here isn't going to yield a one-size-fits-all answer, but it will give you a framework for making the best decision for you and for your family.

This exercise has three primary benefits:

1. It stimulates meaningful dialogue between spouses and helps them "get on the same page."

2. It is a great tool to share with your estate planning advisors so they can tailor your plan to your goals.

3. It can be used to communicate with your children about your intentions and desires. You can do this in person or by letter, but communication can help set realistic expectations.

Forms in Chapter 8 will help you with this exercise.

Step One: Ask All The Right Questions.

Before you and your spouse set an inheritance amount that is appropriate for your family, I suggest you start with some introspection. You might begin with the following thought-provoking questions about your own situation, your children and your current plan to distribute your wealth.

Your Situation

· What is your approximate net worth?

What is the nature of your assets (e.g., closely held business, farmland, commercial real estate, life insurance, securities)?

· How old are you?

· What is your estimated life expectancy?

· How would you describe your relationship with your children?

· What type of lifestyle do you live?

Your Children

· How old are your children?

· Are they all from the same marriage?

· Are they single, married, divorced?

· What career paths have they taken?

· What type of lifestyle did your children grow up in?

· What level of financial maturity have they exhibited to date?

· How have they handled any significant cash gifts you have given them?

· Are they savers or spenders?

· Do you meet with your children regularly?

Distribution Plans

· Do you intend to leave an equal amount to each child?

· Do you intend to transfer significant assets to your children during your lifetimes or only upon your deaths?

~ If at death, will you give to them outright or in trust?

~ If in trust, when will your children ultimately receive the assets?

Step Two: Clarify Your Intentions.

Most people are quite clear on what they do not want their children to spend their inheritances on. The most common items include:

· Support a drug or illegal substance habit

· Gambling

· Prostitution

· Extravagant lifestyle

· Ability to avoid engaging in a meaningful career

· Payments to a divorced spouse

They are not as clear, however, about how they do want their children to spend their inheritances. The following list includes some common acceptable items, but it is by no means exhaustive. Add your own items to it.

$ _____	New(er) Home
$ _____	New(er) Car
$ _____	Graduate School
$ _____	Debt Reduction
$ _____	Grandchildren's College Fund
$ _____	Retirement Fund
$ _____	Jewelry, Artwork, Collectibles
$ _____	Foreign Travel
$ _____	Country Club Membership
$ _____	Vacation Home
$ _____	Investment Fund
$ _____	"Do Whatever You Want" Fund
$ _____	_____
$ _____	_____
$ _____	_____
$ _____	Total

Step Three: Quantify Your Acceptable Item List.

After you have identified the type of items you would like your children's inheritances to purchase, place a dollar amount or range next to each item. Total these numbers. It is important for spouses to agree on both the items that appear on the list and the dollar amounts.

Step Four: Compare Before To After.

Gaining a shared clarity with your spouse about exactly how much you wish to leave your children is a giant step in the planning process. The next step is to determine whether your current estate plan achieves those goals. To do so, ask your advisors to prepare a flow chart that illustrates who gets exactly what under your existing plan at each of your deaths. Compare the result with the goals you and your spouse have set.

Visualize how things will go under your current plan as if it were a movie: Does your current plan reflect the values you hold as parents? Does it have a happy ending? Many people are surprised by the discrepancy between the goals they identify using the *How We Would Like Our Children To Use Their Inheritance* Worksheet and the operation of their current estate plans.

If the amount parents calculate using the Worksheet is less than they expect, some people decide to increase the amount of the inheritance they will leave to their children. Many parents, however, discover that their existing estate planning documents provide their children with more than the total amount they calculated on the *How We Would Like Our Children To Use Their Inheritance* Worksheet.

Whether the total amount you calculate is more or less than you expected is not the point. The important thing is that you consciously make an informed decision about how much money to leave your children. Once you've made that informed decision you can develop a plan to prepare your children to receive the amount you desire and communicate with them about how you'd like them to use it.

Put It All Together.

Studies confirm that most wealthy individuals want to pass some of their wealth to their children but are concerned that leaving them too much money may be counterproductive. Knowing what the right amount is can be difficult to determine and is very personal.

If you want to leave money to your children, I hope that this exercise will help you clarify your motives for doing so. I am confident that the exercise will provide you insight into answering the "How much?" question for your family. Most importantly, the exercise puts you in charge and removes you from default planning mode. Finally, by thoughtfully answering the questions and inserting dollar amounts, you give your advisors the guidance they need to adjust your plan and documents to accomplish your goals.

Studies confirm that most wealthy individuals... are concerned that leaving too much money may be counterproductive.

ONE "ENOUGH" QUESTION AND FOUR DIFFERENT ANSWERS

The following stories illustrate how four sets of parents dealt with the how-much-to-leave-the-kids question. One relied on traditional (or default) planning to maximize a child's inheritance and minimize taxation without preparing the child to handle sudden wealth. Others took creative steps outside of the default-planning mode to prepare their children to receive inheritances of both money and family values. The first story is about a father who did some great tax planning, but failed to instill his values in his son and communicate his wishes to him.

In the second story, two sisters with the same estate planning goals used very different strategies to meet their personal/family goals.

In the third story, a couple increased their giving to their three sons as their knowledge and maturity around wealth grew.

The last story involves a father who made it his second career to make his adult children financially literate and increased the amounts he left both to his children and charities.

The Case Of The Failed Inheritance

"Max" was a hard-charging guy who spent his entire career building a commercial storage business. Like many of us, he was no fan of taxes and dreamed that one day, his only son "Mitch" and possibly Mitch's children, would inherit and run his business. So, upon the recommendation of his tax advisors, Max began to aggressively transfer shares of his company to Mitch. Max initiated this strategy when Mitch was in grade school and continued it for more than 20 years.[4] When Max died unexpectedly at age 62, Mitch's interest in the storage business was worth several hundred million dollars.

Mitch, now age 30, stepped into the role of president and owner, and two years later stepped out of it—selling the company for cash.

Free from the "drudgery" of owning a business, Mitch devoted himself to spending his father's fortune. He began commuting between his multi-million-dollar homes on his private jet accompanied by various girlfriends and groupies. In essence, he retired in his 30s to a life that his father would not recognize, much less approve of. Today Max's son lives a life of the spoiled playboy. Nothing about what happened was part of Max's dream. In fact, it was truly Max's nightmare.

I find that "failed" inheritances are almost always attributable to a lack of communication. Too often, parents give money to children with no direction and then are disappointed in how children spend the funds. It's been my experience that most children will follow the wishes of their parents if those wishes are clearly communicated to them. A short story illustrates my point.

---

[4] *I believe it is important to distinguish between making Annual Exclusion gifts of cash ($15,000 per person in 2021) and gifts of non-voting stock in a family business. To pass a family business to successive generations it is often essential to gift stock consistently over many years to the next generation. Not making lifetime gifts of company stock can result in unnecessary taxation that can threaten the future viability of the business. There are two important differences between gifting shares in a business and making cash gifts. First, owning stock of a company typically brings no voting rights and the stock cannot be liquidated. Second, the parent/business owner normally works side-by-side with those children active in the business as a mentor with the opportunity to pass on values regarding wealth and money.*

Same Goal, Very Different Outcomes

Two sisters, "Jennifer" and "Elizabeth," ran an advertising agency. They had inherited the agency when their parents died in a tragic car accident years before. The two young women poured their hearts and souls into that business, building it into a regional dynamo over a 20-year period.

Having accumulated more net worth than they had ever imagined, Elizabeth and Jennifer sought the advice of a reputable estate planning attorney. This attorney pointed out that upon their deaths, each estate would have to pay significant estate taxes. To minimize that liability, he suggested:

· Purchasing life insurance on their lives to both fund a buy-sell agreement and create a source of cash to pay the estate taxes.

· Beginning the transfer of wealth to their children to reduce the value of the sisters' estates and shift wealth to the next generation.

His reasoning was that since the children were the ultimate beneficiaries under the sisters' estate plans, why not transfer assets to them now and let the assets appreciate in the children's estates?

The attorney advised Jennifer and Elizabeth that, under current law, each could make Annual Exclusion gifts of as much as $15,000 per year to each of their children. If their husbands also participated in the gifting, they too could give $15,000 to each child. Over years, the sisters and their spouses could transfer significant wealth to their children without paying any taxes.

Jennifer and Elizabeth had similar family situations: both were married, and each had two children. In approaching their legacies, however, they tailored their own plans.

Elizabeth and her husband immediately began to give their children the maximum allowable amounts. At Christmas, each *child received checks for $30,000 and an explanation that the gifts were part of their parents' "tax planning."*

After four years of "Christmas giving," Elizabeth and her husband returned to see their attorney for an estate plan check-up. When asked how the gifting program was going, Elizabeth shared that she was very unhappy with it. "The kids have blown it. They have used the money to buy fancy jewelry, take exotic trips with friends and buy designer-label clothes." Elizabeth had lost some respect for her children and was frustrated with this aspect of tax planning!

The attorney was surprised to hear Elizabeth's story, not because he hadn't heard similar ones from other parents, but because he knew that Jennifer had had a completely different experience. "Why don't you talk to Jennifer about her gifting program?" he suggested.

Elizabeth did exactly that the following day. Jennifer told her how she and her husband had talked, before they started giving, about the goals they wanted to accomplish. In addition to shifting wealth and saving taxes, they wanted to teach their daughters (ages 17 and 19) about:

1. Saving and investing.
2. Spending wisely.
3. Helping others who are less fortunate.

Jennifer and her husband agreed to give $30,000 to each child each year, but decided to place those gifts into three buckets:

Bucket 1: *An "investment" account that the children owned but that Jennifer controlled via voting rights. The purpose of the LLC was to hold investments that the family would make together.*

YEAR	INVESTMENT	LIFESTYLE	CHARITY	TOTAL
1	$20,000	$5,000	$5,000	$30,000
2	$18,000	$6,000	$6,000	$30,000
3	$16,000	$7,000	$7,000	$30,000

Bucket 2: A "lifestyle" account to hold funds for the children to spend on items they wanted.

Bucket 3: A "charitable" account from which the children could disperse funds to the charities they chose.

Jennifer explained to Elizabeth that she and her husband met with their children every six months for two to three hours to discuss the gifting. They reviewed the investments and performance. Each child reported on how she had spent funds in her lifestyle account and which nonprofits she had decided to contribute to.

"The kids are learning about the basics of investing, saving, and giving, but we're learning what's most important to them through their lifestyle choices. We're also learning which causes they are passionate about," Jennifer told her sister. "We look forward to these meetings and are so proud of how both are learning to handle money responsibly."

Elizabeth (like Max) had done everything right from an estate planning standpoint. Both had effectively transferred wealth and reduced their tax liability. Jennifer, however, had used tax planning as a platform for teaching her children valuable life lessons. In doing so, she gained peace of mind knowing that when her children receive their inheritance, they are likely to have the skills, maturity, knowledge, and experience to be prudent stewards of her estate.

Perhaps the best way to communicate your desires for your children is to put them in writing, then reinforce those wishes verbally on a consistent basis. Families that have had the best experience are those who make a conscientious effort to pass on their values through regular family meetings focused on financial education.

This communication can take many forms. Think of the level of communication as a spectrum. You'll need to decide where you want to fall on the spectrum. The lowest level of communication is to leave a typical estate plan to be read only at your death. The children will assume that they are free to do whatever they decide with their share of inheritance.

The next level of communication is to write a personal letter to your heirs spelling out your desires and hopes. Children can then reference the letter in the future when pondering, "I wonder what Mom and Dad would have thought of this?"

A higher level of communication is to write a letter and talk to your children during your lifetime to clearly spell out your intentions.

The highest form of communication is best illustrated by two stories from our CAP® class speakers. In the first, we meet parents who incorporated charitable giving into the values they wanted to pass to their children.

Sowing And Reaping The Seeds Of Responsibility

"Ralph" and "Susan" had three sons. Ralph ran a very successful franchise business. Through stock options and prudent investing over many years, they accumulated a sizable estate.

When their sons were teenagers, Ralph and Susan decided to teach them financial literacy. Each year, on the day before Thanksgiving, they would meet for two to three hours. Ralph always prepared an agenda. It was age appropriate and changed each year. The early meetings focused on things like: saving for something they wanted (a bike, a stereo, a car, etc.); how compound interest worked (both for and against you); how to effectively use a credit card; how to save a portion of each paycheck. As they took jobs (part-time in college and full-time after college), the agenda included withholdings from paychecks (FICA, Medicare, federal and state income taxes, medical insurance, etc.), 401(k) plans, auto and homeowners insurance, mortgages, etc.

When all the boys were out of college, Ralph suggested the boys and Ralph prepare personal financial statements and compare them. At this time, Ralph and Susan began making significant cash gifts to their sons each year. The meetings then began to focus on how to invest, how to finance a home, how and when to incur debt and how to minimize income taxes.

Because the boys were accountable each year to compare their personal financial statements, they maintained family budgets and exercised financial discipline. The more responsible they became, the more money Ralph and Susan gifted them. They helped their sons save for their children's college education funds.

Today, the boys are in their forties. All are doing well. They still meet annually with their parents, Ralph and Susan. The agendas today focus on estate planning and charitable giving. Ralph and Susan have made it clear they feel they have given their sons enough. The balance of their estate will be left to various charitable causes.

A portion of Ralph and Susan's gifts each year is contributed to a donor advised fund at their local community foundation in each son's name. As a part of each annual meeting, each son reports on where his charitable dollars were distributed and why that charitable cause was important to him.

The annual pre-Thanksgiving Day meeting now is broken in two one-hour meetings. The first hour is just Ralph and Susan and their sons. They focus on personal financial statements and estate planning. The second hour includes spouses and grandchildren. The focus of that meeting is charitable giving.

While Ralph and Susan readily admit few families could compare personal financial statements each year without causing friction and resentment, it worked for them. The sons are all financially successful and truly like each other. Ralph and Susan take great satisfaction in the fact each son now holds a similar annual meeting with his children. After conducting these annual family financial meetings for over 25 years, Ralph and Susan are comfortable in the knowledge their sons will be good stewards of their wealth and are gratified by how the meetings have helped their family grow closer over the years.

Some people feel that, if they haven't taught their children how to handle money by the time the children finish school and move out of the house, it is too late. The following story involves a family whose adult children were out on their own—some living in cities far from their parents—yet who found a way to meet regularly to further their financial education.

Starting Late Is Better Than Not Starting At All.

"Phil" had a background in finance and had served on the executive teams of two very large corporations. When the second company was sold, Phil found himself out of a job at age 63. He had plenty of money and energy, so he decided to "retire" to a second career. Part of that "career" would be to provide his four adult children the financial education necessary to prepare them to ultimately receive a sizable inheritance.

Phil gathered his four children (one son and three daughters between the ages of 30 and 40) and explained his plan. The family would meet every six months for one full day. The meetings would be on Saturdays, start at 8:00am and finish after lunch. They would then spend the afternoon at their home and conclude with a dinner. Phil would pay the travel costs for children who lived out of town. Each child received a $500 board fee for attending.

Phil had made many contacts over his years in finance. He called upon some of those contacts in his new "career." For each semi-annual meeting, he prepared a written agenda sent out in advance. Topics included a wide range of items dealing with finance.

1. *Banking (how the FDIC works; securing the highest rate and lowest charges; how to borrow money effectively; establishing a line of credit, etc.);*

2. *Investing (definitions of financial instruments, mutual funds, asset allocation, taxation, money manager fees, risk-adjusted returns) and explaining how the stock market operates;*

3. *Insurance (auto, homeowners, liability, life, disability, long-term care, commercial);*

4. *Taxation (income, payroll, federal, state, estate, inheritance, sales);*

5. *Accounting (personal financial statements, personal balance sheets, personal budgets, W-2s, K-1, 1099s);*

6. *Estate planning (wills, trusts, powers of attorney, living wills); and*

7. *Professional advisors (which ones you need; ways they are paid; how to use them effectively).*

Phil covered some of the topics himself and often invited former colleagues, advisors, and vendors to address his children as well. When the guest speakers completed their presentations, Phil and his children would speak among themselves about what they learned. They would ask questions about how topics affected them personally.

Phil's wife, "Mary Ann," sat in on every meeting. She had never expressed an interest in financial matters because Phil always handled their personal finances. However, Phil wanted Mary Ann to learn more about finance in the event he were to die before her or become incapacitated. With their children in the room, Mary Ann was more open to learning.

After lunch, Mary Ann always organized a group activity, e.g., touring a museum, hiking in a park, going to a movie, watching a football game on television, playing a board game. The important thing was they spent those two days together every year.

Phil was able to use his knowledge and the contacts he'd made over the years to provide a financial education to his children. The children made a gift of their time to their parents and siblings. Together they grew stronger as a family.

After nearly 10 years of semi-annual meetings, Phil and Mary Ann felt comfortable sharing their personal financial information and estate plans with their children. They have placed their assets in trust and have their children serve as trustees. When Phil and Mary Ann pass away, there will be no surprises. The children know what there is, where it will go, how it will be managed, etc.

As the children learned more about finances and the parents gained more confidence in them, the amount Phil and Mary Ann decided to leave them increased.

As an interesting side note, after meeting for about five years, Phil and Mary Ann gifted $1,000,000 to an investment fund owned entirely and equally by the four children. The bylaws stated that the children could take distributions as needed, so long as all four children unanimously agreed. Phil was pleasantly surprised; no distributions were ever taken. Apparently, whatever pressing needs the children had were not so pressing after all! Today, the fund has more than doubled in size and continues to appreciate.

When presenting to our CAP® Study Group class, Phil brought two of his daughters. Group members asked them about the value of the semi-annual meetings from their perspective. Neither had a financial background and both admitted that some of the topics discussed were "above their heads." However, they said they are much more confident about money and finance and grateful for the education. Both have started mini meetings with their small children to teach them the basics of personal budgeting and saving. Both agreed that what they cherished most about the semi- annual meetings was the quality time spent with their parents and siblings. They hope to continue the tradition even when their parents are no longer able to lead them.

A Commitment Of Time

This chapter started with the question, "How much should I leave my children?" The lists that followed were designed to help you answer the question of why you would want to leave them any money at all. Once you considered all the reasons that you might want to provide an inheritance, you encountered several challenging questions to help you "back into" the dollar amounts that are appropriate for your family. Finally, you met four people who dealt with the question of legacy for themselves and their children.

The common theme to all stories, except Max's, is that all these parents wanted their money to do more. These parents did more than go to their attorneys' offices every few years to update their estate planning documents. They committed significant personal time and energy to talk to their spouses, examine their motives, meet with their children and communicate with them about financial matters.

...there is simply no substitute for clearly and regularly communicating your intentions through both your words and actions.

If you want to be confident that you are leaving your children enough, but not too much money, and that they will use that money in accordance with your wishes, there is simply no substitute for clearly and regularly communicating your intentions through both your words and actions.

Finally, if you are tempted to dismiss the possibility of passing on your values because you think you or your children are too old to start now, or that you don't have enough financial knowledge to conduct family meetings, or that your children are too set in their ways, too distant or simply uninterested, you may be right. Family meetings are not for every family. But you may be wrong. Family meetings can be very effective, and there are people who can help you organize them: your financial advisors, certain community foundations and non-profit professionals. Before you decide whether family meetings will work for your family, I urge you to keep an open mind as you read the chapters related to charitable giving and conducting family meetings (Chapters 5 and 6, respectively).

CHAPTER 5

Preparing Children To Receive An Inheritance

There are only two lasting bequests we can give our children,
one is roots, the other wings.
STEPHEN COVEY

Preparing Heirs: Five Steps to a Successful Transition of Family Wealth *and Values* by Roy Williams and Vic Preisser is arguably the most comprehensive data-based, longitudinal study ever conducted on the transfer of wealth within families. Over a 25-year period, Williams and Preisser interviewed 3,250 families of means about their family's transfer of wealth. Their conclusions were stunning: OVER 70% OF WEALTH TRANSFERS FAILED! A "failed" transfer occurred when beneficiaries involuntarily lost control of the inherited assets.

The typical causes of an unsuccessful transfer were foolish expenditures, inattention, incompetence, litigation expenses, taxes, bad investments, and family feuding.

Having spent my career helping high-net-worth families transfer their assets to their children through sophisticated estate plans, I found it hard to believe that 70% of the plans I had helped clients implement failed! The tax advisors I worked with were quite competent, so was it possible that we had made that many mistakes?

Williams and Preisser's study provided the answer: less than 3% of the "unsuccessful" transfers were caused by technical error such as the attorney's drafting of the documents or providing poor tax advice. Rather, the study concluded, "The single most important issue that undermines successful transfers of wealth is *the breakdown of trust and communication within the family unit.*[5] (Italics are mine.) The next biggest problem is the lack of preparation of the heirs. As advisors, we never dealt with this issue! Frankly, we never really thought about what happened to the wealth after we figured out how to pass it to the children.

In retrospect, I suppose the reasons for failure shouldn't be too surprising. The first time many of the heirs learn about the extent of their parents' wealth is upon their parents' deaths. Children typically have no experience managing money and simply do not know what to do. While standing under a sudden deluge of money can be invigorating, it can also be overwhelming. Heirs are left to figure out how to manage the shower with little or no guidance.

"The single most important issue that undermines successful transfers of wealth is the breakdown of trust and communication within the family unit."

Modern Estate Planning

Unfortunately, in the nearly 20 years since the publication of Williams' and Preisser's study, I have not seen any marked improvement in the percentage of successful wealth transfers. As I see it, the problem is the estate planning process itself. Tax attorneys are the ultimate creators of estate plans. While I acknowledge that other advisors play an important role (e.g., accountants, financial planners, life insurance agents, trust officers and wealth managers), it is the attorney who drafts the documents.

---

[5] *Preparing Heirs: Five Steps to a Successful Transition of Family Wealth and Values by Roy Williams and Vic Preisser*

Tax attorneys do what they are taught and paid to do: 1) save taxes; 2) preserve as much wealth as possible and 3) help individuals maintain as much control over their wealth as they can. When the final documents are signed, witnessed, and delivered to a client, lawyers feel their job is done. They put clients on a calendar to update the documents in three to five years. When death occurs, the attorney will probate the client's estate. Will the heirs handle their inheritance responsibly? That question is given virtually no thought, and the 70% failure rate will likely continue.

...the definition of insanity? "Continuing to do the same thing, over and over again, and expecting different results!"

What is the definition of insanity? "Continuing to do the same thing, over and over again, and expecting different results!"

Tax attorneys aren't the only professionals doing little to prepare heirs; other financial advisors have little to no training in preparing heirs and are not compensated for doing so.

What then can be done about the 70% failure rate?

Shift The Estate Planning Paradigm.

It is time for a paradigm shift in how we view the estate planning process. We can no longer walk out of our attorney's office, put the newly signed documents in a safe deposit box, and hope for the best! We need to step up! We need to accept responsibility to prepare our heirs to use the money we will leave them to enable them, rather than cripple them. And we need to begin now.

Our country, as mentioned in Chapter 1, is in the largest inter-generational transfer of wealth in history. Furthermore, the wealth gap in our country continues to widen. According to U.S. Federal Reserve data collected over the last 30 years, total U.S. net worth has become increasingly concentrated in the top 10 percent. This trend has accelerated since the Great Recession that began in 2007, and again after the Covid-19 pandemic of 2020. (In 2020 to be in the top 10%, your net worth had to be roughly $1,300,000 and to be in the top 1%, your net worth exceeded $11,000,000.)

Those in the top 10% have benefitted from large investments in publicly traded securities. However, the bottom 50% of the population owns virtually no corporate stock and accounts for only about 2% of our country's net worth.

The wealthiest 1% of Americans possess 40% of the nation's wealth; the bottom 80% only 7%. Why is this relevant? Due to an increased concentration of wealth, lower estate taxes and an aging population, those fortunate enough to be heirs will receive even larger inheritances, sooner!

It is essential that we accept the responsibility that comes with great wealth and provide direction to our children.

Without proper guidance and training, these super-sized inheritances may prove detrimental to our heirs. It is essential that we accept the responsibility that comes with great wealth and provide direction to our children.

In the balance of this chapter, I will summarize several potential sources of "heir guidance" then give you some ideas to apply to your family.

A PARENT'S WEALTH RESPONSIBILITY TOOLS

The Financial Services Industry

The trends I mentioned above: greater concentration of wealth, lower estate taxes and the demographics of inter-generational wealth transfer have not gone unnoticed by our country's leading financial institutions. The largest banks all have private banking services that cater to their well-heeled customers. They, of course, want to include money management as part of a comprehensive banking relationship. To attract clients and position themselves to retain clients into the next generation, many now offer training for beneficiaries by in-house consultants with expertise in family dynamics. Depending on your banking relationship, this service might be a source of information for your family.

The popularity of DAFs is growing at a double-digit rate...

The largest investment firms (Fidelity, Vanguard, Schwab, etc.) dominate the field of charitable donations, specifically donor advised funds (DAF). Here's a quick summary:

· DAFs allow donors to establish and fund an account by making irrevocable, tax-deductible contributions to a charitable sponsor. Donors then recommend grants from the account to charitable organizations.

· DAFs are uniquely positioned to accept non-cash assets such as publicly traded securities, real estate and even closely held stock.

· When assets are gifted to a DAF, the fund immediately liquidates the assets. The liquidated assets then remain in the fund until the donor recommends that grants be made to other charitable organizations.

At the end of 2019, 53 national charities had DAFs with 731,110 accounts holding total assets of $87.23 billion. The popularity of DAFs (not just those offered by financial institutions) is growing at a double-digit rate, making up over 12% ($38.81 billion) of all individual giving on an annual basis.[6] It is likely by 2022 there may be over $100 billion under management just within these financial institutions' DAFs.

Recall that approximately 75% of America's wealth is held by baby boomers and their parents and that the bulk of deductible charitable contributions are made by individuals over 55, with most coming from those over 65.

---

[6]*National Philanthropic Trust, The 2020 DAF Report, https://www.nptrust.org/reports/daf-report/*

So why are large investment firms in the charitable donation business? That's simple:

1. They know where the money is.

2. They know the people holding the wealth have charitable inclinations.

3. Someone must manage the funds within a DAF until the grants are made. Who better to do so than these financial institutions?

As the story of the grandmother who invited her grandchildren to form a board of directors designed to pass her values and teach them the joy of giving to those in need will illustrate, charitable giving can play an important role in training one's heirs about the responsibilities of owning wealth. (See Madge in Chapter 6.)

While these financial institutions and other national charities now hold over half of all assets in donor advised funds, other sponsors include single issue charities such as universities, Jewish federations, specific issue charities (e.g., social justice, international relief, the environment). The most common sponsors of donor advised funds are community foundations. In 2019 there were over 600 community foundations with over 83,185 separate donor advised funds holding over $40.22 billion in assets. Like large banks and financial institutions, many community foundations now offer consulting services to their donors. Some of these services include moderating family meetings if they include a philanthropic component.

These organizations are all "following the money." If you already work with one of these financial institutions, you might look to them as a source of information. Don't be afraid to reach out to them to ask if they have resources that might help you in your mission to raise responsible children while creating a legacy for your community.

Educational Opportunities

In addition to looking to financial institutions for advice on educating our children to handle inheritances responsibly, there are an increasing number of articles, podcasts, TED Talks and seminars on the subject.

Professional Organizations And Advisors

Professional advisors can earn additional professional credentials (i.e., CAP® or Chartered Advisor in Philanthropy) and obtain continuing education credit for seminars and classes related to charitable giving. The Purposeful Planning Institute holds an annual three-day educational program for allied professionals who work with wealthy families in their efforts to raise healthy, responsible heirs.

These organizations understand the implications of this massive wealth transfer and are making a difference in the battle against the way estate planning has been done for many years.

Ultimately, the outcome in the battle to change how wealth is passed to our heirs and shared with our communities, depends on us.

Ultimately, the outcome in the battle to change how wealth is passed to our heirs and shared with our communities, depends on us. We, as holders of the wealth, must take personal responsibility for preparing our children to be good stewards of the inheritance they will receive. Let's now review some of the methods families who understand and accept the responsibilities of wealth are using to fight the good fight.

Conversations

While talking to our children about money may seem an obvious step in the right direction, unfortunately, it's a step too few of us take. Like talking to our adolescent children about sex, talking about money is uncomfortable! When is the best time? What is the right age? What level of detail should we include? What if they tell their friends or cousins?

In conversations about money, we also must choose whether the conversations are one-on-one or with all children simultaneously. Should we include in-laws? Do children need to know exactly how much we make or how much we're worth? Will they think we are rich?

Will they now expect handouts? Will knowing they will one day receive a significant inheritance discourage them from working their hardest and giving their very best?

To avoid this unpleasantness, too many parents close their eyes, cover their ears, and put their heads in the sand! The fear of raising children who feel entitled paralyzes us into inaction. The result of our inaction is predictable— the 70% failure rate continues.

Initiating a conversation with heirs

Initiating a conversation with heirs...is the first step in accepting responsibility for wealth.

about your wealth, your plans and your expectations is the first step in accepting responsibility for wealth. Ideally, conversations are face-to-face between just you and your child. If you are simply not comfortable "going solo," ask a trusted advisor for help. Alone or with backup, the key is to start talking about your wealth!

Letters

Writing a letter to your children that they can read upon your death is something I encourage everyone to do. That letter will likely be a treasure your child will cherish forever.

Typically, parents write about how proud they are of their children and how much they love them. You might explain why you are leaving an inheritance and what you hope they do with it. I can assure you that your children are far more likely to follow your wishes when you express them in writing in a loving way. Some parents eventually share their letters with their children before they die.

If you are simply not a writer, I've provided a couple of examples in Chapter 8 to get you started. Alternatively, you might research "ethical wills." One reasonably priced option is *www.personallegacyadvisors.com*.

Family Meetings

In my opinion, the best way to prepare your children to receive an inheritance is through regular family meetings, so I devote the balance of this chapter to that topic.

Hoping and burying one's head in the sand will not prepare your children to receive an inheritance! Holding regular family meetings, however, is a strategy that can create children who are responsible guardians of their inheritance. I won't tell you holding regular family meetings is easy because preparing your children, like anything worthwhile in life, takes time, energy, and patience. I will promise you, however, that family meetings are hugely rewarding!

If you decide to hold family meetings, do some initial preparation, then just do it.

Many parents like the idea of family meetings. They imagine their children looking forward to getting together, listening and learning from them, and sharing stories, laughter and memories with their siblings.

Unfortunately, these blissful thoughts can dissolve as doubts begin to set in. What if my children don't want to come? Will they think holding family meetings is a stupid idea? What if they don't get along during the meeting? Where would we have the meeting? How long should it last? Who will lead it? What should the agenda be? Should we invite their spouses?

It is normal to experience doubts about any new venture we initiate. As in most endeavors, the most difficult step is the first one—committing to holding meetings. If you decide to hold family meetings, do some initial preparation, then just do it.

Once you decide to hold family meetings, there are five logical steps you can take to make your meetings effective.

FAMILY MEETING PREPARATION

Step 1: Set Your Goals.

Perhaps the most important first step to holding successful family meetings is to be clear on your reasons for holding the meeting in the first place. Your goals are unique to your family, and you may have one goal or many. Whatever goals you set, put them in writing and prioritize them. Only once you know what you hope to accomplish do you communicate your goals to your children. The key is to be clear with yourself and your children about what you are trying to accomplish.

Here is how one family I worked with prioritized its goals.

- **Build** a forum where we might develop stronger loving relationships with each other so we can work well together when we must make difficult family decisions.

- **Pass** on to our children our personal values through stories and experiences.

- **Share** with our children some of our personal financial and estate planning decisions.

- **Provide** the financial education our children need to be good stewards of the inheritance they will receive.

Step 2: Choose A Meeting Facilitator.

If you decide to hold family meetings, someone must lead them. Will you do it yourself, ask one of your children to run meetings or engage an outside professional to work with your family?

Professional Facilitation: If you love the idea of regularly holding meetings as a family, but don't really want to do it yourself and can afford it, I encourage you to hire a professional facilitator. They can help you clarify your goals, establish the format, draft a mission statement, manage the process, constructively engage all family members, and follow through on any action items. Professional facilitators can be particularly helpful when a family business is involved and/or there exist some strained relationships or dysfunction in the family. Some families get along well but simply want to outsource the meeting facilitation. Whatever your motivation, engaging a professional facilitator is a great way to jump start your family meetings.

If you have never hired a trained family coach, a good place to start your search is The International Coaching Federation (ICF). They have members world-wide. Their coaches must meet stringent educational and experience requirements and display a mastery of coaching skills. A little on-line research (*www.coachingfederation.org* 888.423.3131) should help you identify multiple qualified candidates from which to choose.

Do-it-yourself Facilitation: If you feel comfortable hosting and facilitating your own family meetings, the next steps provide some practical tips to enhance your chances of success.

Step 3: Create The Meeting Format.

· **Prepare** an agenda. Once you determine your goals, you can create the agenda for the meeting and determine which of your children you will ask to take meeting notes and record decisions.

· **Set** ground rules. For example: Will you allot time to each child to speak? Can speakers be interrupted? If so, for what purposes? How long will meetings last? Must cell phones be turned off?

· **Consider** expenses. If travel is involved, will children pay their own travel expenses to attend meetings, or will you reimburse them? Some families pay a "Board of Directors" stipend to offset travel expenses and encourage attendance. (A little financial incentive may kick-start your children's enthusiasm for meetings and keep them coming back!)

· **Decide** whether (or not) to include in-laws. Most families choose to include only children during their initial family meetings. After several meetings (or however many it takes to establish a rhythm), they add in-laws. This choice depends on your family's dynamics, relationships and the individuals involved. My best counsel on this topic is: Go slowly.

· **Create** a file for each child to store meeting agendas, minutes, notes and any required follow-up information. You will find a certain degree of formality will let everyone know this is serious business and they should take it seriously.

· **Give Together** If charitable giving is one of your agenda items, consider inviting each child to donate a sum of money (that you provide) to a charity of their choosing. During a family meeting, you might ask children to share with the group why they chose to give to the organizations they did. In this exercise parents and children learn much about each other's values and passions.

Step 4: Communicate With Your Children.

When you propose the idea of family meetings to your children, you will share with them your goals for holding meetings in the first place. Then:

- **Ask** each child for his or her preferences on dates and times for family meetings. Everyone has limited time. You are competing with their careers, spouses, and your grandchildren's soccer schedules and school events.

- **Accommodate** your children's needs. If one of your children lives abroad or too far away to make travel practical, remember technology is a wonderful thing. Better to hold a meeting via Zoom or FaceTime than hold no meeting at all.

- **Invite** each child individually to the family meeting and ask for their help in making meetings successful.

- **Send** a written agenda to children in advance of each meeting.

- **Thank** each child after meetings, in writing, for attending, and remind them of any follow-up actions and the date of the next meeting.

Step 5: Improve Your Odds.

Through experience, I've found that parents can assume attitudes that will improve the odds that the family meetings they hold will achieve their goals. These include:

- **Be flexible.** If you don't complete the entire agenda but meet some (or all) of your goals, you've succeeded!

- **Be patient.** Just because you hold a well-planned "formal" meeting, participants do not suddenly behave differently or check their personalities at the door. Your son who speaks before he thinks or daughter who is sensitive to any perceived slight will behave no differently in a family meeting. All of us, especially children, are works in process. Children are maturing and that takes time.

· **Expect disputes.** It is perfectly normal for siblings to disagree and for children to disagree with parents. Harsh words can be part of the process of reaching decisions and part of family life, but they need not set the tone. Model the behavior you expect from your children and use a reminder of your goals to bring everyone back on track.

· **Share responsibility.** Success depends on both you and your children so allow them—no, direct them—to assume leadership roles as appropriate.

Every family has its own unique dynamic. You may have one child or ten. They may live next door to you or be dispersed throughout the world. Some may get along with their siblings better than others. Children may be married, single, divorced, or have life partners. It doesn't matter. All that matters is that they are your children.

Family meetings that include teenagers will obviously be different from those involving a 50-year-old child. If you are widowed, your family meeting will not be the same as one hosted by a couple. That too doesn't matter. You simply need to start from where you are today.

Have fun. It's all about the journey!

MY FAMILY'S MEETINGS

My first experience with family meetings was a personal one. It began years ago with a family corporation. First, some background. My mother and father were both raised in the Midwest, each in large Catholic families of very modest means. During grade school, my father was hired out to a neighboring farm and never had the opportunity to attend high school. Neither attended college, nevertheless, through years of hard work my father built a successful automobile dealership. When the lifetime exemption was $600,000 and the top estate tax rate 55%, my dad's tax advisor encouraged him to begin gifting assets to his eight children to avoid paying estate taxes. While my father had no intention of giving up lifetime control of his money, he abhorred the idea of paying federal estate taxes. Reluctantly, he set up a family corporation. He and my mother held the only voting shares. Each year, through annual exclusion gifts (of up to $10,000 per child), they transferred non-voting shares to their children.

My father asked me to run the corporation's annual shareholder meetings. In the early years, meetings lasted only about an hour during which my father did almost all the talking. He reported on how the business and investments had performed that year. There wasn't much discussion.

Then a funny thing happened. As we became familiar with both the format and our parents' expectations, we began to relax. We started asking questions about our parents' estate plan. The meetings began to stretch out to two, and sometimes three, hours. After the initial "business" portion of the meetings my mother and father would often tell us stories about their younger years—stories we'd never heard before. Soon everyone would share childhood memories. In my family there is a 22-year gap between the youngest and oldest siblings. Meetings provided an opportunity for us younger kids to get to know our older siblings. Inevitably, there was much laughter, and occasionally a few tears, as we shared each other's triumphs and pain.

Our family meetings continued for over 20 years. My parents scheduled the meetings just before the annual Weber Family Reunion held each summer. (We recently held our 50th annual family reunion!) The strong bonds of trust we built in those annual meetings served our family well. Friends and acquaintances marveled at how well we got along when our parents died and as we settled their estate.

While our family meetings started out as a formal corporate procedure, they turned into much more. They provided us financial education. We learned about borrowing money, interest rates, taxation, depreciation, investments, insurance, lease agreements, employee benefits, dealing with bankers and much more. While my parents had always lived lives of frugality, modesty and hard work, family meetings provided them the opportunity to talk about why those values were important to them. Our family meetings were the one opportunity we had to talk as adults without the distraction of grandchildren or spouses. We grew in our friendship as siblings. Our family meetings became a sort of "glue" that brought and held our family closer together.

ANOTHER FAMILY'S MEETINGS

Not too long ago an acquaintance told me that she had tried a family meeting, but "it didn't work." I asked her to tell me more.

Meeting Failure Or Lesson Learned?

"Louise" asked her attorney to help her with her first family meeting, so he sent a letter inviting her four children to meet in his office at the time he and Louise had chosen.

At the outset of the meeting, Louise announced that her attorney would tell the children about her estate plan.

The attorney spent about an hour explaining the technicalities of Louise's estate planning documents. When he finished, he asked if the children had any questions. The youngest timidly raised her hand and asked a question. Her older brother jumped in and answered the question in a way that made her feel silly for asking. His response had the predictably chilling effect and inhibited any further questions. With no questions to ask and nothing else to add, Louise called the meeting to an end. She left disappointed about the lack of interaction and dismayed that her children didn't get along better. She wasn't sure she would try another family meeting.

How might this situation have turned out differently?

Clarify Goals. The only goal Louise set for her attorney was to share her estate plan, yet she was disappointed when the meeting accomplished that goal. Obviously, she had other goals, but she didn't communicate them to her attorney or to her children. Be clear on your reasons to hold family meetings (e.g., financial education, passing on values, family camaraderie, etc.).

Seek Input. Louise set the meeting time and date based on her schedule and that of her attorney instead of asking her children which dates and times might work best for them. She unwittingly chose the same date as her son's annual golf game with his high school friends. Not surprisingly, her children (and especially her son) viewed her "invitation" as a mandate. If Louise holds future meetings, she might seek her children's input on both dates and agenda.

Personalize the Invitation. Louise let the attorney issue the invitation instead of personally inviting each child face-to-face or by phone. She failed to share with them her intent and hopes for the meeting. She never asked for their help in making it successful.

Meet in a Comfortable Setting. She didn't realize that meeting in an attorney's office can be off-putting and stifle an informal flow of conversation. I would have suggested that she hold the meeting in her own home or in a vacation home.

Use an Informal Format and Keep It Interesting. Louise's attorney viewed this meeting as he would any other client meeting: He dressed and acted the part. If you invite a professional advisor to a family meeting, ask them to dress casually and let them know that you want them to be engaging, informal and facilitate discussion.

Keeping it interesting can be a challenge once meetings have become routine. Here's one technique that a couple used to keep their children engaged in family meetings both during their lifetimes and (they hope) after their deaths.

Keep It Interesting.

"Sandra" and "Alex" began holding family meetings a few years ago with their three adult children. They called to ask for my help. They had just finished their fourth annual family meeting and while the meeting went well, they were running out of ideas to keep the meetings fresh. We got together to brainstorm and came up with what we feel will be an exciting meeting next year.

For next year's meeting I convinced Sandra and Alex to make a gift of $15,000 to each child, a total of $45,000. Each child will receive three separate gifts of $5,000 each. They will be used as follows: The first $5,000 may be spent by the child for anything they desire. The second $5,000 will be deposited in a brokerage account in the child's name. The third $5,000 will be contributed to a donor advised fund established in the child's name at the local community foundation. Sandra and Alex committed to continue the gifts for three years after which they would reevaluate.

To add a little "spice" to their meetings the children will compete to see who can invest the $5,000 deposited in their brokerage accounts most effectively and accumulate the largest amount at the end of the 36-month period. The winner will receive a $5,000 winner's bonus! All funds will be distributed at the end of the contest. At each meeting, each child will have to detail what they learned about investing during the last year.

The funds contributed to the community foundation can be distributed to any charities selected by the child. However, at each meeting, each child will have to report which organizations they selected, why they choose them, and what result they hoped their gift might have.

One child will take responsibility for the investment portion of the meeting and another child the charitable giving portion. The third child will facilitate a new part of the meeting by asking each participant the following question, "What is one of your fondest memories of our family and why does it make you smile?"

Sandra and Alex are pumped about next year's meeting! The children will be surprised to be receiving the cash gifts. Sandra and Alex are excited about the teaching moments that should present themselves. I am excited that they understood the need to keep the meetings fresh and fun. Regardless of how the details work out, I am confident they will grow closer as a family and learn to trust each other even more.

The last thing I encouraged Sandra and Alex to do is to amend their estate plan to form an entity (limited liability company) upon their deaths and fund it with enough cash that the children can continue to hold family meetings and have their expenses paid for from the new entity. Sandra and Alex have already created the structure and begun the tradition. By providing the funding, they will enhance the chances these meetings may go on for many years after they are gone.

As Louise discovered, the first family meeting may not meet all expectations, much less be a resounding success. Don't be discouraged. Family meetings are new to you and your children. Admittedly, formal meetings about topics you may never have discussed with your children can be somewhat uncomfortable, but if you openly share the reasons for holding them and what you hope to accomplish, your first meeting could be the start of a process and discussion that will last many years.

WHAT'S IN IT FOR THE KIDS?

We've talked about all the great reasons parents hold meetings, but what motivates children to participate? When we first initiate family meetings, I think it is always helpful not just to communicate our goals but also to appeal to our children's self-interest.

When we first initiate family meetings, I think it is always helpful not just to communicate our goals but also to appeal to our children's self-interest.

We are asking them to give us their time, so we can expect them to ask themselves, "What's in it for me?" Giving them money, funding grandchildren's education and giving to their favorite charities are three topics that usually get our children's attention.

Annual Gifting. If you decide to make gifts of cash or assets to your children, the family meeting can be an ideal place to do it.

Education Funding for Grandchildren. If you choose to fund all or part of your grandchildren's college expenses (i.e., 529 Plans, trusts, etc.), the family meeting is a good time to talk about funding, investment results, tax consequences, grandchildren's college intentions, etc.

Charitable Giving. Many families include charitable giving as a standing meeting agenda item. Discussing charitable activities can be enlightening, heartwarming and a great way to learn about each other's passions.

...the key to a successful wealth transfer is to build trust...

MEETING TOPICS

At the end of this chapter and at *SpectrumOfLegacies.com*, you'll find a list of financial topics that you might include in your family meetings. I encourage you to add topics that are appropriate for your family.

For example, if you are a 70-year-old widow and your children (ages 45 and 40) are financially savvy, your meetings might focus on investments in specific assets and estate planning issues. Alternatively, if your meetings include grandchildren and your intent is to educate them on how to accumulate and preserve wealth, your topics, delivery style and level of detail would be dramatically different. You will want to clearly define what you hope to accomplish and tailor your topics and approach to the financial sophistication of your children/grandchildren.

Keep in mind that not every meeting has to focus on financial issues. Many families choose non-financial topics for some of their meetings. They understand that the key to a successful wealth transfer is to build trust and improve communication between family members. You might consider incorporating one or more of the following topics into your meetings.

Personality Tests

Businesses often administer "personality tests" to their management teams to improve understanding and communication among team members. Two of the most well-known tests are The Myers-Briggs Type Indicator and Gallup's StrengthsFinder. Each takes less than 30 minutes to take online. Families have used these assessments as a fun way to recognize the different styles and strengths among family members and provide a common vocabulary when working on the family's collective communication skills.

Genealogy

Having one or two family members trace the family's history and share their findings can reinforce how much family members have in common and strengthen the family bonds.

Site Visits

When families incorporate charitable giving in their meetings, they may visit some of the nonprofits that they support. Visits can be a fun bonding experience.

Family Stories

Some families will include the opportunity for each family member to relay a memory they have of a family experience or why they are proud to be a member of the family.

Sharing stories can build trust and improve communication within your family. The gift of your time and the sharing of your stories may ultimately be a more important gift than the money you plan to leave them.

MEETING TIPS

I suggest that you begin and end meetings on a positive note, so family members leave with a positive impression of their time together and see value in working together.

To start meetings, you might ask each person to give brief answers to the following questions: "What is going really well for you in your life? What has made you happy recently? What are you really looking forward to in the next six months?"

During meetings you might ask everyone turn to their left or right and tell that person something they appreciate about them.

It is not critical to complete your entire agenda. If your family has committed to regular meetings, you can pick up where you left off at the next meeting.

Some meetings will be more productive than others, especially when family members want to share a story or experience that is unrelated to your topic.

During the last 10 to 20 minutes of a meeting, you might ask questions like, "What do you feel went well today? What is something you will take away from today's meeting that you feel will have a positive impact on you? What is one thing we did right today that you would like us to repeat in future meetings?"

PERFECTION IS THE ENEMY OF THE GOOD.

If family meetings are new to you, expect some missteps and don't be afraid to experiment. Initially, your children may hesitate to talk for fear of appearing stupid in front of siblings and advisors. It takes time and patience to build the trust necessary for open and honest learning to take place.

The most important step is the decision to use family meetings to regularly share ideas, information, and values with your children.

Occasionally, children may disagree with each other and put you in the awkward middle. If one of your goals is to promote family unity, awkward moments are not only a natural part of family dynamics they are great growth opportunities. As a parent, you know that it is more important for your children to learn to disagree agreeably or coax a festering problem out into the open than it is to master the intricacies of insurance or investing. Strong family bonds do more to avoid the heartbreak and litigation that can arise from settling an estate than any expertise in financial instruments.

Logistics are merely details to be worked out. The most important step is the decision to use family meetings to regularly share ideas, information, and values with your children.

Through meetings you create an environment for discussion that is warm and inviting. The gift of your time and the sharing of your "stories" may ultimately be a more important gift than the money you plan to leave them.

Conclusion

Remember why 70% of family wealth transfers fail? The breakdown of trust and communication within the family unit! Keep that in mind. Each time you gather as a family, you have the opportunity to communicate and make a deposit into your family's "trust bank." Family meetings may be the only time during the year you have meaningful dialogue with your children and their spouses with no distractions.

When managed properly, family meetings can be very rewarding as you see your family members work together for common goals. Patience and persistence will be the keys to your success.

TOPICS FOR FAMILY MEETINGS

To create the strongest bonds of trust among family members, there is simply no substitute for in-person, face-to-face meetings. Yet many parents have a hard time even visualizing how they could possibly prepare their children to receive a significant inheritance. The following is a list of topics that I have seen parents use in family meetings to do just that. Again, these topics may not be appropriate for your situation. Once you see how much there is to talk about, however, my hope is that the list gives you the confidence to start your own family meetings!

A few hints:

· When planning your agenda, take a longer view (five to ten meetings) so you don't attempt to cram too much information into too few meetings and overwhelm your children.

· Be persistent and be patient with yourself and with your children. It takes time and practice to build the groundwork necessary to make your children good stewards of the wealth you will pass and time to develop trust among family members.

· Appreciate each child's talents, weaknesses, personality, and contributions. Your family is unique. Your children are unique.

Persistence, patience, and respect for each person puts you on the road to becoming a closer, grounded, well-adjusted family.

Trusts

1. What are they?

2. How and why are they used?

3. What is a trustee?

    a. What are trustee responsibilities?

    b. How is a trustee paid?

    c. Who should be asked to be a trustee (corporate vs. individual)?

4. How we have used trust(s) in our estate plan

    a. Are they funded or unfunded?

    b. Who will be the trustee?

    c. What are the provisions?

    d. When and how can money be distributed from them?

    e. How will the trust be taxed?

Recommendation: Consider inviting a bank trust officer to address your family to explain how they: 1) typically invest money, 2) gather, account for and manage all assets after a death, 3) determine who gets distributions, and 4) have had to decline requests for distributions.

Taxation

1. Ordinary income tax

2. Capital gain tax

3. Transfer taxes

    a. Gift

    b. Estate

4. Step-up in basis

5. Entities including "pass-thru"

6. Taxation of:

    a. Trusts and trust distributions

    b. Qualified retirement plans

    c. Inherited assets

7. Charitable deductions

    a. Lifetime

    b. Bequests

8. Taxes at our deaths

    a. Who pays (apportionment)?

    b. Who figures out all this?

    c. Steps we have taken in our estate plan to minimize taxes

Recommendation: Consider inviting your accountant or tax attorney to address these topics.

Social Security And Medicare

1. What are these programs?
   a. When did they start?
   b. How are they funded?
      Give examples of payroll taxes.
   c. What are the benefits?

2. How does one qualify for benefits?
   a. When should one apply for benefits?
   b. How much will the benefits be?

3. What is a Medicare Supplement policy?

4. How does this affect us?

Recommendation: Consider inviting your financial planner to address these topics.

Insurance

1. Automobile and Homeowners
   a. Our levels of coverage
   b. Our reasons for coverage
   c. Children's levels of coverage

2. Personal Liability Insurance
   a. What does it cover?
   b. How much should someone typically have?
   c. Approximately how much does "typical" coverage cost?

3. Life
   a. What is life insurance?
   b. Why do people have it?
   c. How much should one have?
   d. What types of polices are there?
   e. At death:
      i. How is money (proceeds) paid out?
      ii. Who do proceeds go to?
      iii. How are proceeds taxed?

  f. Can anyone qualify for life insurance?

  g. How much does it cost?

  h. What is the best way to buy it?

  i. Our life insurance

   i. How much we have

   ii. Our reasons for purchasing the type we have

   iii. Consider sharing a story about how life insurance made a significant impact on the life of a family.

 4. Long-Term Care

  a. Define long-term care

  b. How much does a policy cost?

  c. Is it only for very old people in nursing homes?

  d. How does long-term care insurance work?

   i. What are the benefits?

   ii. How long do benefits last?

   iii. How does it pay care providers?

  e. Does the U.S. government pay for care?

  f. Who pays if I don't have enough money?

  g. Actions we've taken to prepare for eventuality of a nursing home stay or need for in-home care

  h. Our preferences and desires regarding nursing home and/or in-home care

Recommendation: Invite your insurance agent to discuss various types of insurance, review your current coverages and answer questions about your policies.

Debt And Borrowing

 1. What is debt?

 2. What are the various types of debt?

  a. How does interest vary by type of debt?

  b. What does it take to qualify?

  c. When and how is debt paid back?

 3. What organizations loan money?

 4. What is a credit score?

 5. How do credit/debit cards work?

6. Incurring debt
   a. When might it make sense to incur debt?
   b. When can it be a poor choice to incur debt?

7. Basic rules of borrowing

8. Our view of debt
   a. How we have used credit to our advantage during our lives or careers
   b. Pitfalls we want to help our children avoid

Recommendation: Share with your children why you feel the way you do about personal debt. This conversation is a great way to pass on your personal values.

Budgeting And Personal Financial Statements

1. Family/Household Budgets
   a. Provide an example (or several).
   b. How are they used most effectively?
   c. Budget apps

2. Personal Financial Statements
   a. Provide an example (or several).
   b. When does one need one?

3. Our tips to make maintaining a family budget and personal financial statement fun
   a. Make it a game.
   b. Build in rewards to celebrate success.

4. How we have used budgeting, saving and investing

Recommendation: If you believe that living within your means and delaying gratification bring their own rewards, talking about budgets presents a great opportunity to communicate that to your children.

Banking

1. Checking accounts
   a. Use for direct deposit of paychecks
   b. Use for autopay accounts, (e.g., utilities, mortgage, credit cards, subscriptions)

    c. Balancing accounts

    d. Tying checking account to budget and financial statement

    e. Automatic transfers to savings

    f. Overdrafts

      · fees

      · email/text alerts

2. Savings accounts
   FDIC insurance

3. Titling bank accounts

    a. Joint vs. single

    b. Impact of divorce

    c. TOD and POD

4. Credit cards

    a. Use

    b. Advantages/disadvantages

    c. Features: free vs. annual fee, points, foreign exchange, etc.

    d. Impact of divorce

5. Online payment systems (e.g., PayPal, Venmo, Zelle)

    · FDIC insurance

6. An Emergency Fund

    a. Importance / use

    b. Size

    c. Location

7. Safe deposit boxes

    a. Use

    b. Authorized renters

    c. Access at death

    d. Our use, keys, contents

Recommendation: If you have a strong relationship with your personal banker, consider inviting them to address your family on these topics and to tell your children what banking relationships you have established.

Electronic Passwords

1. Secure storage

2. Protection
   Access to trusted persons

3. What happens upon death or incompetence?

4. Our passwords
   a. Where they are located
   b. When we feel it is an appropriate time for children to access them

5. Children's passwords
   What steps have they taken to protect their passwords?

Recommendation: You can likely handle this topic yourself. Alternatively, consider asking your children for advice!

Saving

1. Percentage of income
2. Employee 401(k) contributions
3. Employee Stock Options

Recommendation: A financial planner can easily explain the impact of investment return, compound interest, and income taxes.

Investing

1. Money managers
   a. What they do
   b. Methods of compensation

2. Asset allocation / diversification

3. Mutual funds

4. Index funds

5. Time horizon

6. Risk tolerance

7. Taxation

8. Our philosophy

Recommendation: This is a topic that may best be served in "bite sizes." Consider asking your investment manager to address the group if he or she is able to speak in layman's terms!

It is critical to find a good communicator who can explain the fundamental principles of investing without losing the audience in technical jargon. Using specific examples can personalize the topic.

Estate Planning

1. Mechanisms of passing assets at death
    a. Wills
    b. Trusts (See Trust section.)
    c. Beneficiary designations
    d. Titling of assets

2. What happens when someone dies without a will?

3. How are assets taxed upon death?

4. Who pays taxes at our deaths?

5. Estate Plans
    a. How often should one update their estate plan?
    b. Describe your estate plan in as much detail as is comfortable for you.

Recommendation: This topic is best discussed in small parts and should be regularly revisited. The more personalized the examples, the more meaningful the education will be.

Entity Planning

1. Limited liability companies
    a. Function
    b. Use in context of estate planning
    c. Governance (meetings, minutes, leadership, voting rights, etc.)

2. Family partnerships
    a. Function
    b. Use in context of estate planning
    c. Governance (meetings, minutes, leadership, voting rights, etc.)

3. S Corporations
    a. Function

  b. Use in context of estate planning

  c. Governance (meetings, minutes, leadership, voting rights, etc.)

Recommendation: Your attorney is probably best suited to address family members on this complex topic.

Charitable Giving

Most people, even children, are familiar with giving to others in need. Some of your children may not be familiar with some of the techniques and tools of charitable giving.

  1. Tax implications

  2. Donor advised funds

  3. Gifts of assets in lieu of cash

  4. Foundations

  5. Pledges

  6. Split-interest gifts

Recommendation: This is a fertile topic for family meetings and best learned by actual giving. Your children are likely interested in hearing why you give to the causes you've chosen.

Family meetings can educate and create responsible heirs—both critical components of your legacy. We turn now to another legacy component: your community.

CHAPTER 6

Creating Your Legacy

We make a living by what we get,
but we make a life by what we give.
WINSTON CHURCHILL

O nce you are confident that you have "enough" for your future financial security and you've decided how much money to leave your children, you can move on to the question of legacy.

I like to think of legacy as connecting our money to meaning: How will you be remembered after you are gone? Will people be inspired by your generosity to the community and those less fortunate? Will they admire the wonderful job you did raising caring, confident, contributing children? Or will you leave everything to children who will bitterly fight over or squander money they feel they were entitled to? Perhaps saddest of all, will you be forgotten because you really didn't make a difference?

My hope in writing this book is to help you teach your children to be responsible heirs and to leave a legacy to your community. As you may have learned from the stories I've shared so far, the two—responsible heirs and legacy to community—are often linked.

I would argue that your community legacy should never be secured at the expense of your family. In true legacy planning, the two—community legacy and raising responsible heirs—

How will you be remembered after you are gone?

are melded. You may decide to work with your children in your philanthropic efforts or not to directly involve them in your efforts. Either way, you will model the behavior you would like them to emulate. Through ongoing communication and transparency, your children will absorb the lessons you teach.

The stories in Chapter 4 (Jennifer and Elizabeth, Ralph and Susan and Phil and MaryAnn) were about parents who left important legacies to their children. Not only did they leave them money, but they taught their children how to respect each other and work together. Parents taught children how to share their wealth with others less fortunate. These parents didn't simply hope that their children would be financially prudent, get along with each other and be generous. They modeled and consciously taught this behavior during their lifetimes to set a pattern for the way they hoped their children would manage the money they would leave them when they died.

The balance of this chapter is about the legacy you will leave your community. Specifically, I hope to inspire you to give to those less fortunate both during your lifetime and upon death in a way that makes giving more thoughtful and meaningful.

GIVING DURING YOUR LIFETIME

The benefits to you (and to your family should you decide to involve them) of giving to charity during your lifetime are many. So too are the challenges unless you establish a few giving guidelines that we'll discuss in this chapter:

- · Be intentional.

- · Narrow your focus.

- · Understand why you give.

- · Find your passion.

- · Use more than cash.

- · Recognize that it is not just about the money.

- · Use your values to drive your giving.

- · Consider making giving a group activity.

· Give yourself a gift.

· Write your own giving plan.

Be Intentional.

Many people and organizations ask you for money to support their work, and you've written many checks in response. Typically, requests come from someone we know rather than from the charities that are our first choice. While not unhappy that you responded, you probably did not find the process to be particularly fulfilling. Yes, the charities appreciated the cash, but did you wonder if your donation really made a difference?

I suspect that, like most of us, you would write bigger checks if you were really passionate about the cause and certain that your donation had real impact. In other words, many of us are reactive or checkbook givers. Most of our giving is in response to a solicitation whether in person, on-line, direct mail or on television.

You may be ready to transition from "checkbook philanthropy" to "intentional philanthropy." Intentional philanthropy occurs when you give money (and/or time) to a cause you find meaningful, and your contribution is significant enough to make a positive difference. No matter how you think about giving at this moment, intentional giving is a journey, not a destination. Every journey is unique, but all typically involve false starts, wrong turns and dead ends. Each one of those "failures" brings a gift: the gift of experience. Committing to be more intentional about your giving is an important first step on your giving journey. Through experience, you will find what works best for you.

Narrow Your Focus.

Too often people who are incredibly generous with their time and money feel inadequate because they cannot say "yes" to everyone who asks them for money. Whether you have hundreds, thousands, millions or even billions of dollars to give away, it is not enough to meet all the needs. You must narrow your focus. Being intentional about your charitable giving, on the other hand, can be empowering and leave you with the knowledge you've done your best. By developing a focused plan limited to the causes and organizations to which you are most committed and align with your values, you will achieve a new level of contentment and satisfaction.

Understand Why You Give.

Knowing what motivates you to give not only helps you be more effective in your giving but also provides you with greater personal satisfaction. In his book *The Seven Faces of Philanthropy* author, Russ Prince, PhD identifies many of the reasons people give. He points out that one reason is no better or worse than another as each can be equally effective. Prince's book goes into depth on the various reasons providing examples from daily life. They might be summarized as follows:

· Doing good in return ("Repayer").

· Doing good is good business ("Investor").

· Doing good is fun ("Socialite").

· Doing good makes sense ("Communitarian").

· Doing good is a moral obligation ("Devout").

· Doing good feels right ("Altruist").

· Doing good is a family tradition ("Dynast").

Gaining insight into your motivations and those of the people who might join you in your giving can help you achieve a greater sense of satisfaction.

When interviewing some of the successful entrepreneurs turned philanthropists in the class I facilitate, it was fascinating to attempt to get at each speaker's "Why."

While expressed slightly differently by each philanthropist, each felt incredibly blessed. They realized that while their success was a result of hard work, many other factors were involved: the values their parents instilled in them; the country they were born in; the teachers who educated them; the bosses who nurtured and mentored them; the challenges that made them stronger; the support of their spouses; etc. In short, each felt a strong sense of gratitude and therefore, an obligation to give back.

Your motivation may be gratitude. It might be to save taxes or create a forum for your children to work together; fulfill a commitment; or a combination of these or other reasons. Understanding your own motivation can help determine what form your giving might take.

Find Your Passion.

Each of us wants to feel good about how we spend our hard-earned money. We want the best value for our dollar. When making on-line purchases we often read reviews to see what others say about a product. Similarly, when we give to charities, we want assurance that they are using our dollars to deliver the biggest benefit to those in need. Rating services such as Charity Navigator, GuideStar and Charity Watch can provide valuable insight and transparency into the charities you may wish to support.

However, I believe it is possible to be too "business-like" in our charitable giving. While some level of due diligence is necessary, I feel that, for individual donors, passion plays a more influential role in giving than does any third-party assessment. As well it should. If you are thinking about embarking on your giving journey, I encourage you to start small and with those organizations dearest to you. It might be a house of worship, a school, a hospital, a hospice center, or a community garden with which you have a personal connection. Giving should start with your heart, not with a rating service. The following story describes how one donor found his passion.

It's Never Too Late to Discover The Joy Of Giving.

"Genevieve," one of my older clients, asked me to visit with "Henry," a close friend of hers to share with him how several of my clients found joy in giving money away in their later years. She told me that Henry was around 80 years old and had done very well financially but was surprisingly "grumpy" about his finances. His two children were financially comfortable and well established in their own careers. Henry gave them money each year and would leave them a very sizable inheritance through his will. "On the surface," Genevieve explained, "Henry has everything he ever wanted, but he simply isn't as happy as one might expect of someone who, by all standards, has it made."

As soon as I met Henry, we developed an instant rapport. He had been in the investment business and was well-versed in finance. He had plenty of income, and a respected estate planning attorney had recently updated his estate plan. From a financial planning standpoint, everything appeared to be in good order, so I complimented him on his planning and asked him what he hoped to gain by meeting with me.

Sheepishly, Henry admitted "I'm not really sure. Genevieve said I shouldn't be so tight and should be giving away money to charities. But I've never done that! I came from nothing and made it on my own. I just figure everyone should do the same. Plus, I don't really know anyone at any charities. I figure that if I start giving them money, they'll only ask for more! While you seem like a nice enough man, I probably shouldn't have wasted your time."

I sat back, took a sip of coffee and said, "Henry, to be truthful, I took this meeting as a favor to Genevieve. I told her I would not charge for our meeting time. I am enjoying our conversation and, if you are willing to share, I would love to hear your life story."

I asked Henry questions about his background: how he met his wife; how he got started in the business, etc. As he became comfortable and more animated, I began to interject more thought-provoking questions, such as:

· *Who were the people who had the biggest impact on you?*

· *What is your definition of a life well lived?*

· *What would you say is a theme that runs through your life?*

· *What adjectives do you feel best describe you?*

· *What is the legacy you wish to leave?*

Henry thoroughly enjoyed reflecting on his life and sharing his insights with me. Our time together went by in a flash.

It was clear to me that Henry's high school years were formative for him. A math instructor ("Mr. Jennings") taught Henry the love for numbers that led to a successful career. Until his death, Henry had kept in touch with Mr. Jennings. I also learned that before she passed away, Henry's wife had been a teacher's aide for many years at the local grade school because she loved the small children.

When I asked Henry if he kept in touch with his old high school, he admitted he had little contact other than reading the alumni newsletter.

"I recently received a brochure about some kind of STEM program," Henry elaborated, "but I haven't read enough to know what 'STEM' even means!"

I informed him that "STEM" stood for Science, Technology, Engineering, and Mathematics. "STEM is a recent initiative in education to get more kids interested in math and science," I started. Seeing that I had piqued his interest I continued, "You mentioned that Mr. Jennings was one of the most influential people in your life. He sparked your love of math which triggered your successful career in finance. Do you think you might be interested in helping the school raise money if it would do something to honor the memory of Mr. Jennings?"

A smile came to Henry's face as he considered this idea.

I agreed to make a couple of phone calls to see if I could find the appropriate person at the school to reach out to Henry to discuss the STEM program in detail. Henry left our meeting with the promise he would call me in about a month to let me know what happened.

True to his word, a month later Henry met me for lunch. He was clearly in a good mood and couldn't wait to share his news with me.

"An exceedingly kind lady from the school came by the house to tell me about the school and explain the details about the new STEM initiative," Henry started. "Of course, she mentioned that her job was to raise the money necessary to

add a dedicated wing to the school just for kids studying math, science, engineering and computers."

Henry's animation did not dim as he told me that he had agreed to pay for the construction of one of the classrooms. In return the school would build a beautiful display with Mr. Jennings' photo, the years he had taught, and a brief history of his life including the impact he had on his students' lives.

"I'm going to have input on the construction and content of the display, and the school wants to acknowledge my contribution during the formal dedication of the building!" Henry was noticeably excited to be able to honor his favorite teacher.

When we finished our meal, Henry said, "I almost forgot to tell you that after committing to the project for Mr. Jennings, it occurred to me maybe I could do something for the grade school where my wife worked for over 25 years. I called the school, and someone will call on me next week."

While I never met with Henry again, I did meet with Genevieve a few months later. She couldn't wait to tell me about Henry. "I don't know what you said or exactly what's he doing, but he's a changed man!" she raved. "He's busy volunteering on projects at the high school and at the grade school where his wife used to work. But this is the best part, Mark: Henry told me that he never realized how much fun it could be to give away money!"

Unfortunately, there are many Henrys among us—people who have the time and money to give but simply don't give to their communities for myriad of reasons. They tell me:

· I'm not sure I have enough for myself.

· My kids might get mad at me for giving away their inheritance.

· I don't know any nonprofits well enough to be comfortable giving them money.

· If I give to a charity, it'll just ask for more.

· I don't feel strongly enough about any one charity to give it money.

· I don't have enough to make a difference.

Use Assets Other Than Cash.

When responding to a solicitation for a donation, it is normal to think, "Do I have enough cash in my checking account to cover this gift?" Admittedly, cash works best for small gifts. For larger gifts, however, cash can be inefficient. Typically, if you give appreciated assets such as stocks, bonds, mutual funds, real estate, etc., you will achieve a more favorable tax result. More importantly, cash accounts for only about 5% of most donors' wealth. The other 95% consists of real estate, closely held businesses, stocks, retirement accounts and other non-liquid assets. The more sophisticated nonprofits understand this and will help you determine which asset is the most tax-efficient for you to give.

Giving an asset such as appreciated securities can be complicated by the fact that the value of the securities may not coincide with the amount you intend to give the charity. This is one reason why gifts to donor advised funds (DAF) have exploded in popularity. A gift to a DAF allows donors to take the full deduction in the year of the gift. Donors can then choose to distribute the funds of the DAF over a period of months or years. Donors can also choose to make the distributions anonymously if they choose. An example might help.

Four Benefits Of A Donor Advised Fund

"Robert" wanted to make a gift of a highly appreciated security valued at $50,000 to fulfill his commitment of $20,000 to his church's building campaign. Robert first set up a donor advised fund at his local community foundation then contributed the $50,000 security to it. The DAF sold the security and forwarded $20,000 to Robert's church in his name. The community foundation, at Robert's direction, made two more distributions from his DAF of $15,000 each over the next two years: one to a food pantry in Robert's name and the other anonymously to a legal aid society.

By using a donor advised fund, Robert was able to: 1) give an asset that afforded him greater tax benefit than a gift of cash; 2) take a tax deduction for the entire gift ($50,000) in the year he made it; 3) make distributions out of his fund for several years and 4) choose whether to make the gift anonymously or in his name on a case-by-case basis.

It's Not Just About Money.

Throughout most of this book, I share many stories of people of great wealth because it is with this demographic that I have spent my career. And yet, I've learned that, more often than not, there is little correlation between the sense of fulfillment one experiences when giving and the amount of the gift. Without doubt, money talks, and nonprofits need a lot of it to carry out their missions. Time and leadership, however, can be every bit as critical to nonprofits as money.

No amount of money will solve our world's most pressing problems. Judgement, compassion, innovation, and leadership just might. I believe that to be a truly effective giver, you must be more than a "checkbook philanthropist." Get involved. Be the change you hope to bring about. Lead by your example.

Use Your Values To Drive Your Giving.

For a number of years, one of our nation's largest, most prestigious banks has conducted an annual survey of their high-net-worth clients. When asked, "What is the most important thing you wish to leave your children?" the answer is not "money," but rather, "personal values." Your values should drive your giving.

In Chapter 3 (Values-Driven Planning), I explained why clarifying your own values is essential to creating your legacy plan. I strongly encourage you to identify the core values that are most important to you. The chart below lists a few of the types of organization/causes you might naturally consider supporting associated with certain core values.

VALUE	ORGANIZATION
Faith	church, synagogue, mosque
Education	grade/high school, college, scholarship funds

Health	nutrition, physical fitness, hospital
Empathy	food pantry, nursing home, homeless, immigrants
Self-reliance	leadership training, scouting, technical schools

Let me share a story of what one wise matriarch did to pass her values on to her grandchildren.

A Matriarch Passes The Torch.

"Madge" was about 80 years old and blessed with many grandchildren. They were dispersed throughout the region, and she did not see them as often as she liked. She and her late husband ("William") had always been very generous, and she wanted to pass "the gift of giving" to her grandchildren.

With the help of a charitable advisor, Madge announced she was establishing a "board of directors" among her grandchildren. To be on the board, a child must be at least eight years old. Once a child turned 25, they "aged out" and must resign from the board.

Upon joining the board each child was given a packet about the etiquette expected in board meetings. In fact, every child was expected to read Robert's Rules of Order. A president, vice president and secretary were elected for one-year terms. Each child eventually rotated through the offices.

Madge held two board meetings per year: one at her home and the other at her vacation home. The meetings lasted about two hours.

Each meeting started with a brief presentation by Madge's son, the family's bank's president. He would, in age-appropriate terms, discuss the prior year and whether or not the bank made a profit. If the bank did not make a profit, there would be no money to share with those in need.

Madge would typically choose five to six separate causes she wanted to give to each year. The board could choose only three and then decide how much to allocate to each. The causes might include: the zoo, the fire department, the Humane Society, Boy or Girl Scouts, etc. With the help of the charitable consultant, the children went on field trips and/or invited the nonprofits to their meetings.

These meetings have been going on for over ten years. The children have learned there are people and organizations that are not as economically blessed as they are. They learned how difficult it is to decide which organization to give to when all seem worthy. They discovered that when acting in a group they must be persuasive to make their points. They also learned to compromise, cooperate, and disagree agreeably.

The children learned profit is a good thing and provides more to share with others. They are learning the basics of business and good citizenship all while growing closer to their siblings and cousins.

The idea for this board came from an advisor who helped Madge and William complete their estate plan. Once they determined to leave "something" in their wills for charity, Madge asked, "Why do we have to wait until we die?" She immediately came up with the idea of connecting with her grandchildren. With the help of a charitable consultant, they developed the business model for their family charitable giving.

Today two children have "aged out." The youngest is now eight, so all children are or have been on the board. The consultant prepares the agenda, helps facilitate the meetings, keeps the meeting minutes and follows through on action steps. Madge gets to spend time with her grandchildren and takes great pride in watching them grow into a caring, cohesive family.

Obviously, this is a significant commitment of time, energy and money on Madge's part to make this work. I am not suggesting this would work for everyone. By using one's imagination, however, you could develop a plan that fits your own family. Certain community foundations and charitable consultants in your community may be available to help you.

Values Can Bind Families Together.

The following story describes how a father's personal values lead him to make a charitable bequest that ultimately drew him closer to his son.

A Legacy Plan Unites Father And Son.

"Charles" had sent his son, "Michael," to private school from kindergarten through 8th grade. Charles presumed that his son would attend the same all-boys private academy he had for high school. But Michael had other ideas. Michael insisted he was going to a co-ed public school that offered a "magnet" program in world languages. The school attracted students from throughout the school district regardless of residence, social, economic, or racial background.

Charles was not happy with his son's choice. The school was in the inner city, so Michael would ride a public bus each day. Charles didn't know anyone whose children attended this school. Reluctantly, Charles agreed that Michael could attend for one semester on a trial basis. After one semester, however, if Charles and Michael weren't both pleased with the school, Michael would transfer to his father's **alma mater.**

Michael loved his high school experience, excelled in academics, and thrived on the diversity. He made Asian, Hispanic, Black, Jewish, and Muslim friends. Some lived in parts of the city Charles had never visited.

Michael went on to excel in college and graduate school. He could speak several languages fluently and traveled the world for pleasure and business.

When Charles drew up his legacy plan many years later, he listed his top three values as:

> *Knowledge: Charles believed education was the key to finding self-fulfillment.*

> *Independence: Charles felt strongly each person must make their own way in life on their own terms.*

> *Justice: Charles firmly believed that all men were created equal in God's eyes and must be treated with dignity.*

As he thought about the legacy he wanted to leave his community, Charles realized a gift to his son's high school would be consistent with his values. Students who attended this school typically were independent-minded and valued their education. The diversity in the student body meant that teenagers learned and socialized with people different from themselves. Charles understood that this familiarity was a giant step toward acceptance and ultimately social justice.

Charles not only left Michael a generous inheritance in his will, he also created an endowed college scholarship at Michael's high school for one deserving graduating senior. When he shared his plan with his son, Michael was stunned and ecstatic! He proposed to his father that together, they immediately begin to fund the scholarship.

Each year, for the rest of Charles' life, he and Michael attended graduation at Michael's **alma mater** *and presented the scholarship. After Charles died, Michael continued awarding scholarships from the fund his father had endowed. Doing so brought Michael fond memories of his father, of course, but more importantly Michael was reminded of the confidence his father had in him as a young boy.*

Consider Making Giving A Group Activity.

For most of us giving is intensely personal. We don't share with others who we give to or how much we give because somehow it would seem like boasting. Plus, personal finance is a topic we were taught not to talk about in polite society.

Having said that, Madge found great fun in giving with her grandchildren. She got to spend time with them and more importantly she was able to pass on the joy of helping others less fortunate.

Whether you decide to give with your children or grandchildren obviously is a function of your family's dynamics. If multi-generational giving is not for you, there are other ways of giving with others. You might join with a friend or small group that supports the same causes. You might join a "giving circle" to consolidate your gifts and magnify your impact. You might join with an entire congregation to build a new house of worship, etc. Working in conjunction with others toward a shared goal can be a fun and rewarding experience.

We are "pack animals," it is in our DNA. Even the most hard-hearted of us cares about something or someone. Each of us has had help along the way, and it is our obligation to help those who come after us by "paying it forward." You will discover that when you make a gift, you are not just helping the recipient, you also help yourself.

Give Yourself A Gift.

It took me years to recognize that giving to others was a "double gift." Of course, the organizations that receive money are appreciative. The surprise was that I also felt so good about giving! I found that giving is personally gratifying and gives me a sense of purpose. In a sense giving away is giving to myself!

In *The Paradox of Giving: Giving We Receive, Grasping We Lose*, authors Christian Smith and Hilary Davidson, write,

> Those who give their resources away, receive back in turn. ... In offering our time, money and energy in service of others' well-being, we enhance our own well-being as well. In letting go of some of what we own for the good of others, we better secure our own lives, too.

Studies show that volunteering might even help us live longer, healthier lives. Marta Zaraska states in her book *Growing Young: How Friendship, Optimism and Kindness Can Help You Live to 100*, "...volunteering reduces mortality by 22% to 44%—about as much as eating six or more servings of fruits and vegetables each day. What's more, volunteers may have 29% lower risk of high blood glucose, about 17% lower risk of high inflammation levels, and spend 38% fewer nights in hospitals than do people who shy away from involvement in charities."[7]

I had a friend who divorced years ago and became estranged from his only daughter. He lived alone in his apartment, had few hobbies other than reading, and the older he got the more reclusive he became. I tried to encourage him to join me in volunteer activities on several occasions, but he always declined. To my knowledge he never gave any of his money to charity. He died a couple of years ago. I often

---

[7] Zaraska, Marta, Growing Young: How Friendship, Optimism and Kindness Can Help You Live to 100, *Appetite by Random House, 2020, page 166*

wonder how much richer his life could have been had he engaged in the community through volunteer work and giving. He never gave himself the opportunity to feel "the gift of joy" that comes from helping others.

Write Your Own Giving Plan.

Gifts to organizations for which you are passionate based on your personal values are the most rewarding gifts you can make. Identifying your personal values can help you select among multiple worthy causes when you have a limited giving budget—which everyone does! (To help you identify your values, please see Chapter 3 Values-Driven Planning.)

All of us—especially those who are active in our communities, run businesses or simply know a lot of people—are solicited by multiple nonprofits. Developing a personalized giving plan helps us sort through and balance those requests. You may choose to devote your entire time-and-giving budget to just one or two organizations. That's fine. "Going deep" with a single organization can be quite fulfilling and make a meaningful contribution to that nonprofit.

Fair warning: Including family members in your giving increases the number of nonprofits from which to choose. While more giving options can create lively family discussions, it can also generate conflict. Having a well-thought-out giving plan based on common family values can add structure and consistency to your giving and minimize conflict.

You'll find a sample giving plan (Our Charitable Giving Plan) in Chapter 8. A giving plan answers some of the typical questions:

· Why are you giving?

· What values will guide you?

· What will be your primary focus? (Feeding the poor? Sheltering the homeless? Promoting literacy? Treatment for addicts? Helping veterans?)

· What will be your geographic limits? (None? Our country? Your state or city?)

· Will you limit yourself to certain types of gifts? (Annual solicitations?

Multi-year pledges? Capital Campaigns? Endowments?)

· How will you give? (Cash? Appreciated assets to a donor advised fund?)

· Will you give only to large, established nonprofits or do you prefer smaller, start-up nonprofits?

· Will you want recognition for your gifts, or do you prefer anonymity?

· Will you establish and commit to an annual giving budget?

The purpose of your personalized giving plan is to keep you on track. It can be as simple or detailed as you want because it's likely that no one else will ever see it. It will also help you feel less regret when you have to say "no" to worthy causes that are not consistent with your plan.

GIFTS UPON DEATH

Over three-fourths of Americans surveyed indicate they make lifetime gifts to nonprofits. Far fewer make gifts (commonly referred to as "charitable bequests") upon their deaths. In the remaining pages of this chapter, I will address:

· Why more people don't make charitable gifts upon their deaths.

· What motivates people to make charitable bequests.

· How people make charitable bequests.

· My suggestions to you.

Why More People Don't Make Charitable Gifts Upon Their Deaths

The first (and perhaps most surprising) reason that most people do not make charitable gifts from their estates when they die is that most people don't have an estate plan. Over 50% of American's die without a written will! (Yes, you read that correctly: 50%). Without written directions to one's heirs, it is difficult if not impossible, to direct gifts to charity from the grave!

"Mortality salience" is the term researchers use to describe why people put off thinking about death and making wills. If they think about death, much less talk about it, some people fear it will happen. I simply call this way of thinking "avoidance." Closing our eyes and putting our hands over our ears is not going to make death go away! Fearing death is a natural human response. Failing to plan for it is irresponsible.

It is a common adage among estate planning attorneys that the average person spends more time planning their next vacation than their estate plan. In my experience, the biggest reason that people who do spend time thinking about their estate plans don't make charitable bequests is that *they don't think about it!*

Over the course of my career, I have sat in hundreds of meetings with clients and their estate planning attorneys. These meetings can often be intimidating for clients. Admittedly, thinking of one's mortality is, by itself, unpleasant. Attorneys then add to the "unpleasantness" by using words and terminology that are foreign to most people. They bring up, discuss and make plans to manage issues such as divorce, bankruptcy, and spendthrift children. They introduce obtuse tax strategies that clients are supposed to understand and then make what could be life-altering decisions during the meeting.

While clients are wrestling with thoughts of death, trusts and taxes, attorneys will ask a question that catches most of us off-guard, "Do you want to include charity in your plan?" Injecting charity into the conversation is almost disorienting. The common answer is normally, "No," "I don't think so," "We haven't talked about it" or "We'll get back to you." In that one moment, a golden opportunity is lost. If we were able to anticipate and discuss the giving issue before meeting with our attorneys, I am confident that far more of us would include charity in our estate plans.

What Motivates People to Make Gifts At The Time Of Their Deaths?

People make charitable bequests for some of the same reasons they give to charity during their lifetime: a sense of altruism and/or gratitude, a commitment to a cause and/or because of the tax benefits.

There is often, however, a larger, more subliminal reason people give to charity upon death. Researchers call this reason the "pursuit of symbolic immortality." In other words, we pursue something of lasting social impact, something that will live beyond us. In this book, I refer to that something as your personal "legacy."

Legacy (or "symbolic immortality") is often at play when we see the name of a wealthy philanthropist on a building (think Carnegie Hall); or on a foundation (the Ford Foundation or the Bill & Melinda Gates Foundation); or on an endowed scholarship (The Rhodes Scholarship or Nobel Prize). On a local level, we see people put their names on private foundations or donor advised funds. Personally, I find it inspiring when I see someone's name on a building, foundation, or endowment. It makes me want to learn more about the person behind the name.

If symbolic immortality does not motivate you to give, consider what effect your death will have on the charities you've given to so generously during your lifetime. For example, if we consistently contribute $10,000 per year to the United Way, unless we leave a charitable bequest, that gift stops upon our death and the organization must find another donor to replace our annual gift. If we leave the United Way a charitable bequest of $200,000, however, it can invest that $200,000 and generate enough income ($200,000 x 5%) to replace our annual $10,000 in perpetuity. Including in your estate plan a charitable bequest to the charities you've supported for years is a natural extension of your lifetime giving.

How Do People Leave Charitable Bequests?

Giving at death can make a lot of financial sense. During our lifetimes we are building and conserving our financial assets to provide for ourselves during our retirement years when we are no longer generating income. We will not know if we will have enough for our retirement until we get there. By delaying major gifts until death, we will know with certainty we had enough for ourselves and are giving out of our surplus.

Favorable tax treatment can be a strong incentive to make a charitable bequest. Consider an individual retirement account (IRA). When we leave the balance of an IRA at our death to our heirs, the IRS will require them to pay income tax. If your estate is large enough, the IRS might also require them to pay federal estate taxes. As a result, 40% to 60% (or more) of the IRA may be lost to taxes. By naming a qualified charity or DAF as beneficiary of your IRA, no taxes will be due and 100% of the IRA balance can be used for charitable purposes.

Many people own life insurance on their lives typically to provide financial security for a spouse in the event of their premature death. But what if a spouse predeceases the owner of the life insurance, or we accumulate enough wealth that a spouse does not need life insurance proceeds for financial security? Changing the policy beneficiary to a qualified charity or a DAF can be an easy way to leave a charitable bequest.

There are a number of strategies and techniques (e.g., Charitable Remainder Trusts, Charitable Lead Trusts, beneficiary designations, etc.) that make charitable bequests tax efficient and appropriate to your personal financial situation. While these strategies are beyond the scope of this book, your tax advisor will be well-versed in them.

One planning strategy that I feel is underutilized is funding donor advised funds for your children upon your death. The ability to make lifetime gifts is an honor and can be deeply satisfying. Leaving a sum of money (a portion of one's IRA is ideal) to a donor advised fund in your child's (or other heir's) name at your death can be hugely rewarding.

Even if you do not have enough financial surplus to give as generously as you would like to your favorite charities, a DAF is an ideal way to give funds after your death and teach your heirs to be philanthropists.

It is not important that you take it upon yourself to learn how each of these strategies works. It is enough that you decide to leave a charitable bequest and let your tax advisors work out a plan that best fits your needs.

My Suggestion

Do not wait to consider a chartable bequest until you are sitting in your attorney's office and are asked, "Do you want to include charity in your plan?" Instead, go into the meeting knowing which charity(ies) you want to benefit, and a dollar amount you'd like to bequest. You can look to the attorney to help you determine the most tax-efficient manner of making the charitable bequest you have already chosen. Keep in mind, it is your legacy. You must take control.

I encourage you to write your own personalized giving plan to focus your lifetime giving. Join with others when it makes sense to multiply the size of your gift. Experience the joy of giving from your heart to causes about which you feel passionate. Model the generosity you want your children to emulate. Understand the impact giving will have on both your community and your family. Be a leader!

CHAPTER 7

Using Professional Advisors Effectively

Trust takes years to build, seconds to break, and forever to repair.
UNKNOWN

Disruption By Technology

In the last decade, technology has caused major disruptions in the fields of law, accounting, insurance, and investments. Today we can usually purchase the product or service we want from the comfort of our homes, at a fraction of its previous cost.

Consider this, in just a few hours at my computer screen, I can:

· Draft my will for less than $300 (LegalZoom).

· File my federal and state tax returns for less than $100 (TurboTax™).

· Purchase stock with no commission (Charles Schwab).

· Purchase a $1,000,000 term policy, with no medical examination.

Many members of the Millennial Generation grew up with computers and prefer to avoid human interaction. They find it more comfortable and convenient to purchase services and products from their smart phones or iPads. This trend will only accelerate as more and more services become available online.

As noted in Chapter 1, however, approximately three-fourths of the wealth in America is held by baby boomers and their parents. This portion of the population did not grow up with computers. Consider that when Steve Jobs and Apple introduced the iMac, the first baby boomers were already 52 years old! When the first iPhone was released, they were 61! While members of this generation use computers and smart phones extensively, they prefer to interact with humans rather than computers, especially when dealing with their financial matters and important life decisions.

Boomers realize that they are well past the mid-point of their lives. They appreciate that the decisions they make about passing their wealth may have a dramatic impact on their heirs and community. They have never been in this stage of life before, and they don't want to make mistakes. To complicate matters, tax laws are ever changing. There's no app that can tell them how much they will need for their own financial security, how much to leave their children, how much to leave to their community and what values will drive these decisions. Answering these questions requires personal reflection, as well as the insight and wisdom of professional advisors who have helped others make these decisions. Furthermore, boomers want continued reassurance from qualified advisors that they are still on track to achieve their goals. This is best done by face-to-face meetings with trusted advisors.

SELECTING YOUR ADVISORS

Most people—but not all—who have accumulated significant wealth have longstanding relationships with professional advisors. I am surprised when someone does not remember the name of their attorney, accountant, financial planner, or insurance agent. That lapse is understandable when a new advisor has suddenly stepped in as a replacement for a long-time advisor who recently retired or died. Sometimes though, people forget because they do not use their advisor(s) regularly and only then when there is a problem. This only-when-I-need-them mindset is unfortunate and short-sighted. Professional advisors can play a critical role in the choices one makes during the last few decades of life.

In Chapter 2 we discussed some of the benefits of working with advisors during your retirement years. A retirement specialist can give you confidence that you have "enough," and can help you maintain that confidence as you reach your later years. An accountant can help you minimize your taxes. An estate planning attorney is essential to draft your estate planning documents. Other advisors (money manager, insurance agent, trustee) can play vital roles in a variety of situations. While much has been written on how to select the best advisors based on knowledge and experience, I plan to focus on a few topics often overlooked: succession planning, conflicts, and meeting regularly as a group.

Professional advisors can play a critical role in the choices one makes during the last few decades of life.

Succession Planning

Frequently we work with advisors we have known for many years and are close to our own age because it is comforting to rely on those we know and with whom we have a proven track record. "Mature" advisors can provide wisdom and insight that newer advisors simply have not yet acquired. However, when we reach our 70s and 80s, there is a good chance that our long-time advisors will no longer be practicing. Does that mean we should replace our current advisors now with much younger ones? Of course not. What it does mean, however, is that you should require each of your advisors to have their own succession plans. This client hand-off should not occur on the day the senior advisor retires. Ideally, the younger advisor will meet with you and the senior advisor for a couple of years before that day, allowing you to develop a level of trust with the junior advisor. A smooth hand-off is not only beneficial to you but also to the advisory firm. Firms that regularly plan for the retirement of their senior advisors have much higher client retention rates.

Another topic often not discussed is the spouse who is most likely to survive. Unless there is a large age difference or disparity in health, statistically, women will outlive their husbands nearly 8 out of 10 times—and by several years. In my experience, husbands of the baby boom generation frequently take responsibility for family finances and selecting the family's advisors. Often, the advisors they choose are male and close to their own age. When a senior advisor suggests a younger replacement, it is important to ask wives what qualities they want in a new advisor. After all, women are most likely to have to deal with new advisors when an estate plan is updated for the final time. Times are changing and widows are increasingly choosing advisors from among the growing number of bright, young females entering the professions.

Conflicts

Professional advisors are collegial—for the most part. They often interact with each other at continuing education programs and/or when serving other clients. Sometimes however, there is an inherent conflict among them that is not obvious to their clients. For example, you may notice that your accountant has recently begun to make subtle undermining comments about your longtime money manager when the money manager is not present. What you may not know is that your

If one advisor regularly pushes you to switch from your current advisor…be sure you understand what's in it for that advisor and what's in it for you.

CPA's firm recently added a wealth management department, and all members of the firm are expected to introduce their tax clients to that new department.

Similarly, you may have worked with your life insurance agent for years, but when she suggests that you purchase a new policy to pay estate taxes, your attorney interjects that he would like to introduce you to someone else who can help with that purchase. What you may not know is that your attorney has developed a referral relationship or even a commission-sharing arrangement with the insurance agent he is recommending.

When the banker who has handled your account for years suddenly suggests that you consolidate all your insurance and investments with her, you may not know that 1) the bank recently acquired a firm that sells insurance and investments, and 2) part of her compensation now depends on the number of referrals she makes to that firm.

The best results occur when all your advisors work together in an open, trusting environment.

If one advisor regularly pushes you to switch from a current advisor to one whom they recommend, be sure you understand what's in it for that advisor and what's in it for you.

These conflicts will happen more frequently as the financial services industry continues to consolidate. My point is not that these "conflicts" are always bad. Sometimes they can result in superior service and/or lower cost. I bring conflicts to your attention because they are not always obvious. We could all benefit from more transparency in these industries.

I have been blessed to work with some outstanding professional advisors over the course of my career. I have found that top-flight advisors typically make referrals only when asked. They respect their client's choice of advisors and are pleased to work with them. The best results occur when all your advisors work together in an open, trusting environment.

CREATING YOUR OWN TEAM

If you are age 60 or older, you are probably entering what is referred to in the financial planning world as the Distribution Phase of your financial life. (You may have already passed through the Accumulation and Preservation Phases.) In the Distribution Phase the focus is: 1) maintaining a steady flow of predictable retirement income and 2) planning for the distribution of your wealth upon your death. There are many pieces to this puzzle.

In a "normal" Distribution Phase, an individual typically needs the expertise of an attorney, an accountant, and a financial planner. With added complexity, a person may also need the expertise of a life insurance agent, a retirement plan specialist, a property-and-casualty agent, and/or a trustee. Even more complex situations may require the expertise of a business transition expert, a valuation expert, or a family counselor.

These experts are used to working together on projects, such as an estate plan. Once the project is complete, the experts disband and wait to be called upon for the next project. Allow me to suggest that we use advisors differently than we use other service providers.

Anyone who owns a home realizes that ongoing maintenance is a fact of life. This is particularly true if you are as unhandy as the author! One of my prized possessions is a list of reliable vendors: painter, plumber, carpenter, carpet cleaner, etc. We call these vendors only when we have a problem. Many of us use our financial advisors in a similar way. They are "on call" and respond when we call them with a problem.

I am asking you to move beyond interacting with your advisors on an on-call basis for this next phase of your life. Consider forming your own personal "board of advisors." I have helped a number of individuals form their own boards of advisors. Normally a board consists of three core advisors: an attorney, an accountant, and a financial planner. You can invite other advisors to meetings as you need them.

Board meetings:

· Provide your professional advisors the accurate, up-to-date information they need to be most effective. Advisors cannot make an accurate diagnosis without a comprehensive picture of your financial and family situation.

· Should be held at least annually to keep all core advisors up to date.

· Run according to a consistent agenda that includes your values.

· Are most beneficial when held in person. Advisors can see your facial expressions, listen to the tone of your voice, and watch how you interact with others. They can hear your responses to each question and follow up when they need further clarification.

· Are an ideal time to explain and reiterate your personal values. (We discussed values-driven planning in Chapter 3.) By listing your values at the top of every meeting agenda, you keep your team focused on your family's desires.

In-person advisor board meetings are the best way for everyone to get a complete picture of your family's situation. They are also the best way for you to receive coordinated advice that is customized to your situation.

Overall, you want a facilitator who will help the other advisors "play nice in the sandbox."

You may be asking, "Won't having all of my advisors meeting at once cost a lot?" Initially, perhaps, but not in the long run. When you clearly communicate to all your advisors at once, you keep advisors on track and focused on your personalized plan. Rather than using what they think most clients want as a default recommendation, they receive a full picture of your situation. Consequently, you spend far less time and money on adjustments and revisions.

If you decide to form a board of advisors, make your expectations clear.

1. You want them to act as your personal board of advisors.

2. Let them know you expect them to come prepared and to participate in your meeting as they would a traditional board of directors meeting. For example, they should be prepared to discuss how any changes in law might affect you, as well as introduce new planning ideas that are consistent with your values.

3. Give them authority to share openly with each other.

Normally, you would choose one advisor as a facilitator to help you set the agenda, coordinate the meeting time, facilitate the discussion, and follow through on any action items. In my experience, the best facilitator is not necessarily the person with the strongest personality. Rather, look for someone who will act as a "servant leader;" someone who can put their own ego aside for your good and the greater good of the group. Overall, you want a facilitator who will help the other advisors "play nice in the sandbox."

The following story recounts how one of my longtime clients set up her personal board of advisors.

A Husband's Wish Becomes His Widow's Peace Of Mind.

Nearly 15 years ago, "Jake" was dying of cancer. While he had been financially successful during his life, his wife of over 40 years ("Agnes") knew very little about their personal finances. Jake was justifiably concerned for Agnes's financial well-being.

Shortly before he died, we were reviewing his life insurance program when he put his feeble hand on my arm and said, "Mark, promise me you will always look after my wife." Making a promise to a dying man is not something I take lightly!

Following Jake's death, I met with Agnes and asked her about her relationship with their advisors. She said that Jake had used both their attorney and accountant for over ten years. While the advisors' primary relationship was with Jake, Agnes liked and trusted both. I asked her to introduce me and tell them that I wanted to "interview" them.

Once Agnes made the introductions, I met separately with each advisor, explained that I wanted to form a "Board of Advisors" and suggested that we meet regularly with Agnes. While initially a bit skeptical, they agreed.

We began meeting quarterly. I brought in a professional money manager to serve on the Board. My staff and I prepared the agenda and took minutes. The Board reviewed all aspects of Agnes's financial life, including: budgeting, cash management, banking, estate planning, insurance (life, homeowners, automobile, liability), property management, investment management, income taxation, charitable planning, educating her grandchildren, Social Security, Medicare, bill paying and communicating with her adult children. Each meeting lasted between 90 minutes and two hours.

Occasionally, Agnes was approached by a vendor of some sort or asked for a sizable charitable gift. She would bring each request to her Board of Advisors. We would analyze that request in the context of her overall plan, then Agnes would make her decision.

Agnes was afraid of "making a dumb decision" or being "taken advantage of." Having her Board as a filter gave Agnes confidence that she was making sound decisions. (Her Board also gave her a great excuse to say "no" when friends or family asked for a loan or handout!)

After nearly 15 years of quarterly meetings, we were running out of things to talk about. Agnes had followed all our recommendations. She had transferred significant assets to her children (but retained lifetime control). She had provided for her grandchildren's education. She had made significant charitable gifts to causes dear to her. Her estate plan was totally up to date. Her investments were diversified and performing well. In short, Agnes was in "maintenance mode."

When I suggested we cut back to just semi-annual meetings, Agnes looked me straight in the eye and asked, "Mark, do you know what the most frequent topic is when I have lunch with other widows my age?" I admitted that I had no clue. "Money!" she said. "We all live in fear that we could run out of money one day and be dependent on our children or destitute the next day."

Before I could object, she continued, "I know intellectually that I have plenty of money, but emotionally, I occasionally still get worried. Those worries disappear every time we meet. I walk out reassured, grateful, and confident." She added, "Mark, I don't care about the fees. I consider them to be an 'insurance premium' for my feeling of financial security. Your fees are a small price to pay for knowing, really knowing, that whatever happens, whether I become incompetent, or even if I die, everything will be taken care of. You give me peace of mind."

With Agnes's speech the light bulb popped on in my mind! When we get to retirement age, most of us continue to use professional advisors in the same way we did before we retired. We wait until we have a "problem," then we call an advisor to "fix" it. As advisors we act in nearly the same way: We react like firemen. We wait until there's a fire, and we put it out!

When your friends begin to worry about all the things that can go wrong with their finances as they age and your children wonder if your financial house is in order, your personal board of advisors can help you and your children maintain confidence in your financial situation. If at any point you feel that your financial ship has gone off course, you know that at least once per year you and your advisors can "reset." Confidence comes from the experience of success repeated regularly.

MEASURING SUCCESS

I have been active in legacy planning since about 2012. I have facilitated Chartered Advisor in Philanthropy (CAP®) Study Groups, read, written about, and addressed numerous groups on the topic, but mostly, I have been learning about and from the amazing number of professional advisors who continue to "blaze the trail" and help their clients leave meaningful legacies. I will talk more about a few of them in a moment.

As a result of my study of legacy planning, it occurred to me recently that perhaps we should reconsider how we measure the success of our professional advisors. Allow me to explain. Historically, it seems to me that "success" for advisors means completing a task accurately, on a timely basis, and at a reasonable fee. For example, I want my accountant to file my tax return and help me minimize the income taxes I pay. I want my estate planning attorney to prepare documents, so my property passes to the people I want to receive it in the most tax-efficient manner possible. I want my money manager to grow my assets into the largest nest egg possible while incurring the least amount of fees. I want my life insurance agent to find the policy with the greatest benefits at the lowest price. Success is tied to the advisor's current actions, *not to the result of those actions*. Perhaps a story best illustrates my point.

Judging Our Plans By Their Results

During one of the CAP® Study Groups I facilitated, I interviewed "Glenn" a former CEO of a major company. (Glenn is not his real name, of course.) Glenn had started right out of graduate school as a management trainee. Over his 40-year career he climbed the organizational chart to become one of the company's most successful CEOs.

I asked Glenn, "With the benefit of your experience, what is the single most important piece of advice you would give a new management trainee today?" He paused to collect his thoughts and said something totally unexpected.

"I would tell her that you will only be as successful as your people." He then elaborated, "Assume that you will not be promoted until you have recruited and trained your replacement to be better than yourself. Act as if your success within the company will be based on not just your own performance, but also on the performance of those you trained and mentored."

That was profound! Can you imagine how successful that company would be if every manager's performance were based on not only his own performance but also on those for whom he was responsible?

After that meeting, I pondered whether we could apply Glenn's sage advice to professional advisors. What if professional advisors were judged not simply on how much of their clients' monetary wealth they were able to pass to children, but on whether children deployed wealth in accord with their parents' values? If that were the case, I suspect that advisors would urge their clients to make their children aware of the wealth they would be receiving well before they received it. They might establish an "heir training program" and act as mentors. Advisors would meet regularly with the children to make certain they clearly understood

What if professional advisors were judged... on whether children deployed wealth in accord with their parents' values?

their parents' values and were well prepared to be good stewards of their inheritance.

Now I am not naïve enough to believe it is practical to pay professional advisors based on the ultimate results of their clients' planning. But what if the public were to judge the success with which we (the wealth holders) pass wealth in the same manner? In other words, "success" would mean that our children were good stewards of their inheritance, becoming good community citizens and sharing with those less fortunate in the community?

Today various organizations keep track of how much money individuals accumulate, (e.g., The Forbes Fortune 400 lists the 400 wealthiest people in the world.) Many people revere those who have amassed the most: The bigger their pile of money, the more "successful" we deem them to be. But what if we were judged not by how much we accumulated, but how well we trained our heirs to be good stewards of the amount we left them and how much we (and they) gave to our communities? The answer is obvious. Our current practice of "dumping" our life's fortune on our heirs at our deaths with no training would fall into disfavor. Once we accepted responsibility for how our wealth is used in the future, we would focus more on what happens after we are gone. That shift would not be easy. It would take time and effort, but the result would be a far better world.

TRENDSETTERS

A growing number of professionals are leading the way in this new field of legacy planning.

Philip Cubeta is a professor at The American College of Financial Services who directs its Chartered Advisor in Philanthropy (CAP®) program. Phil is a pioneer in integrating charitable giving into a multi-disciplinary curriculum. Over 2500 advisors and non-profit professionals from across the country have earned the CAP® designation and incorporated the philosophy into their law, accounting, financial planning, and nonprofit practices. I first encountered many of the ideas I have shared with you in the CAP® curriculum.

John A. Warnick is a highly respected Denver, Colorado estate tax attorney who founded the Purposeful Planning Institute. Each year he hosts a national conference for hundreds of advisors from the estate planning and ancillary fields with the purpose of redirecting the focus of these professions from primarily tax avoidance to legacy or "purposeful" planning. Over the last two decades, John has created a network of dedicated professionals intent on helping people leave meaningful legacies. The impact he is having on purposeful planning will be multi-generational.

David R. York is an estate planning attorney in Salt Lake City, Utah who has developed a unique way for individuals to engage in values-driven planning. In his firm, a full-time, non-attorney counselor meets with clients for several hours before they meet with David. The counselor elicits each person's story and personal values (and sometimes includes a client's children in portions of their meetings) in an effort to define and clarify the family legacy parents wish to leave. David prepares documents only after he has heard a client's story and understands their values. It is this type of innovative thinking that will change the practice of estate planning.

Susan Turnbull of Boston, Massachusetts and author of *The Wealth of Your Life: A Step-by-Step Guide for Creating Your Ethical Will* holds workshops to help people write their own "ethical wills."

Russell James, III, JD, PhD, CFP® is a Professor of Charitable Financial Planning at Texas Tech University and a prolific author and speaker. Arguably the foremost expert in the country on charitable bequests, Dr. James has generously shared his insights on increasing charitable giving with me and innumerable nonprofits. His spirit of sharing is characteristic of the advisors leading the way in this field.

In this book, I am synthesizing much of what I have learned from these and other trendsetters as well as from the many highly successful individuals I have interviewed.

Integrating values with estate planning is a growing phenomenon. It will take time for widespread change to occur, but I am optimistic. You can play a part in accelerating the pace of change by selecting professional advisors in your community who have specialized training in legacy planning. The greater the demand for this type of planning, the more available it will become.

CHAPTER 8

Building Trust
Through Communication

*Building trust is a process. Trust results from consistent
and predictable interaction over time.*

BARBARA M. WHITE

In Chapter 5 we learned that nearly seven out of ten wealth transfers fail, and the single most important cause is the breakdown of trust and communication within the family unit. In second place is the lack of preparation of the heirs. I devoted several pages to holding structured, regular family meetings because I firmly believe that there is no substitute for meaningful face-to-face dialogue. Not everyone, however, wants to hold family meetings. Some people feel more comfortable writing letters that children can keep and reread for many years. Other people do both as my wife and I do: hold family meetings and write letters to their children.

The letters in this chapter developed from letters my wife and I have written to our children and to others. My wife and I have been married for over 40 years, have five wonderful children and ten grandchildren. All have taken different paths in life, live in different parts of the country, and all are successful in their own ways. We could not be prouder of them. We have shared and discussed our letters with them.

Your family is just as unique. Perhaps you have just one child or multiple children from multiple marriages. Perhaps you are divorced or widowed and have never remarried. You could be close to one child and estranged from another. It doesn't matter. These letters are simply templates: Take what is helpful, modify them to meet your needs and ignore the rest.

Similarly, the worksheets are designed to clarify your thinking, engage you in intentional planning, and then share with your advisors so they can tailor their advice to your goals. I hope you find them to be helpful.

My wife and I have been holding family meeting with our five adult children and their spouses for several years. We hold two meetings per year—each lasting about three hours. We hold one in-person meeting in the summer during the weekend of our wedding anniversary and the other remotely the weekend before Thanksgiving. We created a standing agenda that works for us. We do not include all the topics listed on the Topics for Family Meetings in Chapter 5, but some families do. Your family meetings will evolve into a format that works best for you.

This chapter is meant to provide practical hands-on tools you can readily adapt to your family's needs. If the templates provided resonate with you, feel free to download them from *SpectrumOfLegacies.com* and personalize them to meet your needs.

The materials are presented in three sections:

1. Letters To Your Children

2. Letters To Others

3. Worksheets For You And Your Advisors

SECTION 1: LETTERS TO YOUR CHILDREN

No two families are exactly alike. We express our feelings and communicate with one another in our own unique ways. The following letters attempt to translate much of the content of this book into personalized communication with adult children. The style and tone of these letters may not be consistent with how you speak to your children. That's fine. Take the themes and revise them using your own voice. These letters are meant to inspire you to author your own letters.

These letters are not legally binding and are not a substitute for formal, attorney-drafted documents. They are meant to supplement those documents and provide a human touch to otherwise sterile documents. Your children will keep these letters and read them over and over, just to "hear" your voice.

I suggest that you keep these letters with your formal legal documents and share them with your advisors. Many people prefer to let their children "discover" these letters when their estate is probated. Others choose to share them with their children while alive as a platform to discuss their intentions and hopes. The choice is yours.

This section includes:

1. Introduction To Our Legacy Plan

2. Our Obligations And Values

3. Why We Established Trusts For You

4. Our Family Meeting Fund

5. Why We Included Charitable Giving In Our Legacy Plan

6. What You Can Expect To Receive From Our Legacy Plan

Introduction To Our Legacy Plan

This letter establishes the foundation for the other letters in this section and your estate planning documents. It describes your expectations and the reasons you've chosen to distribute your property in the way you have.

||||||||||||||||||||||||||||||||||||||||||||||||||||||||||||||||||||||||||||||||||||||||||||||||||||||||||||||||||

Dear children,

Your mother and I recently updated our estate planning documents. Although we are in excellent health and hope to live for many years, life is unpredictable. While our documents explain how our assets are to be distributed, it is our intent to explain why we structured our estate in the manner we did.

Parents teach their children by both their words and actions. Our estate planning documents will be our last "lesson," and we want them to reflect our values.

In "broad brush" terms, our estate plans leave our property upon our deaths to each other. Only upon the death of the second of us will property pass to you. You will each receive an equal share of a specific dollar amount. The balance will pass to our charitable fund. This letter provides insights into the reasons for our decisions.

Both your mother and I were blessed to grow up with wonderful parents in loving families. While our parents met all our needs as children, when we finished our schooling, they made it clear that we were to make our own way in the world. When we had our first child, your mother wanted to be a stay-at-home mother. Since she had a good job and I had only just graduated, our decision put a financial strain on us. Our family grew more quickly than our business, so we had little discretionary income in the early years. We had each other, our friends were in a similar situation, and we had fun making do with the little we had. Your mother and I made a pact: She would run the household and raise our children and I would provide the necessary financial support. Without doubt, your mother had the harder job!

Without your mother's support I would never have enjoyed the success I've had in business, so the primary goal of my estate plan is to make certain she has absolute financial security for the remainder of her life. Because I have complete confidence in her judgement, my trust documents give her significant latitude while still being tax efficient and protecting our assets from creditors and predators.

One of the wonderful gifts our parents gave each of us was a college education. We didn't truly appreciate the value of that gift until we put you through school. It was only then we realized the huge financial sacrifice our parents had made.

Just as we have helped you through college, we also want to help your children. We will continue to fund 529 Plans for each of our existing (and any future) grandchildren.

Perhaps the greatest gifts our parents left us were the examples of hard work and living within one's means. They gave us the freedom to fail and the opportunity to make it on our own.

Over the years, we have witnessed the impact that inherited wealth can have on heirs. While some children are equipped to handle the inheritance of large sums wisely, the impact on children who have little preparation or instruction can be hugely detrimental. These recipients often lose their self-esteem and tend to overcompensate by buying big homes, fancy cars, expensive jewelry and living an extravagant lifestyle, some abusing alcohol, sex, or drugs.

A short story that best exemplifies this phenomenon is the story about a butterfly.

A man found a cocoon of a butterfly. One day a small opening appeared. He sat and watched the butterfly for several hours as it struggled to force its body through that little hole. Then it seemed to stop making any progress. It appeared as if it had gotten as far as it could, and could go no further.

The man then decided to help the butterfly. He took a pair of scissors and snipped off the remaining bit of the cocoon. The butterfly then emerged easily, but it had a swollen body and small, shriveled wings.

The man continued to watch the butterfly because he expected that, at any moment, its wings would expand to support the body, and the body would contract.

Neither happened! In fact, the butterfly spent the rest of its short life crawling around with a swollen body and shriveled wings. It never was able to fly.

What the man, in his kindness and haste, did not understand was that the restricting cocoon and the struggle required for the butterfly to get through the tiny opening were God's way of forcing fluid from the body of the butterfly into its wings so that it would be ready for flight.

Sometimes struggles are exactly what we need. If God allowed us to go through life without obstacles, it would cripple us. We would not be as strong as what we could have been. We could never fly!

On the many occasions when we were tempted to give you money for things you really wanted, we knew it might bring us joy in the short-run but would be detrimental to your growth in the long-run. It is for this reason that we have made a conscious decision not to give you large cash gifts while we are alive.

It is statistically likely that one or both of us could live a long time, and you could be near retirement age before you receive an inheritance. For those of you who didn't accumulate adequate funds for a comfortable retirement, your inheritance will be your ultimate safety net. Those of you who were more adept at accumulating wealth can pass your inheritance to your children and grandchildren or give it to charity.

Upon our deaths, a sizable portion of our estate will go to charity. Specifically, that portion will be left to our existing donor advised fund for the following reasons.

- As spelled out in a separate letter, we feel that we have met our obligation to you, and the inheritance you will receive will provide an adequate safety net.

- Giving to charity is something we have done our entire lives and is consistent with our values.

- Allowing you to make gifts from our donor advised fund should be rewarding and provide you an opportunity to meet regularly and work together.

In conclusion, we hope that this and the following letters will shed light on what is important to us and why we have chosen to distribute our assets in the manner we have.

- We value education as an opportunity to broaden our minds and add value to society.

- We believe in hard work, self-discipline and the self-esteem that come from making it on one's own.

- Through judicious use of trusts, we feel we have provided you both protection and flexibility.

- By providing you a predetermined amount of inheritance, we believe we have been generous while providing you incentive to do your absolute best.

- We have purposefully delayed your inheritance to provide us maximum lifetime financial security and provide you the opportunity to make your way in the world on your own terms.

- We believe in giving back to those less fortunate and using charitable giving to build stronger family ties.

We realize our plan is not perfect. No doubt we have failed to anticipate certain actions or circumstances. Please accept any mistakes we may have made, and know that we have done the best we can with the tools and knowledge we have. Our plan will be successful if it allows you to reach your full potential and is not a detriment to your personal growth.

Living a life that matters isn't a product of luck or circumstance but of choice. It is our sincere hope that you choose to live a life that matters, and our estate plan helps you to achieve that end.

Love,

Mom and Dad

Our Obligations And Values

Today many parents feel obligated to pass all their wealth to their children, and children feel entitled to receive all of it. This letter describes the obligations some parents feel they have to their children and the values that guided them in life and in their legacy planning.

⁣‖‖‖

Dear children,

As we began to plan our legacy, we thought about what we felt we "owed" you as your parents. After much contemplation we arrived at this list.

When you were a small child, our obligations were to:

· Nurture and love you.

· Provide you a safe environment (warm healthy meals, a home free of abuse, a kiss and a hug each night before we tucked you into a clean bed).

· Send you to school each morning and help you with your lessons.

· Be your primary role models.

When you were a young adult, our obligations were to:

· Let you try and fail without permanent consequences.

· Help you build confidence, self-esteem and humility.

· Educate you through high school and college.

· Model love for each other and respect for yourself and others.

· Encourage you to always give your best effort.

Now that you are an adult, our obligations are to:

· Provide a welcoming, loving home to which you may always return.

· Emotionally support you in your own life journey.

· Pass on wisdom and advice when asked.

· Lovingly welcome your life partner into our family.

· Love and cherish your children.

Perhaps you noticed that leaving you a large financial inheritance is not on our list of obligations. That is because we have chosen to share our financial resources with you—during our lifetimes and upon our deaths—out of love and gratitude, not from a sense of obligation. We are proud of the adults you have become, each finding your own path and supporting yourselves.

The foundation of our legacy plan is made up of the core values that guide us and that we hope we instilled in you: accountability, humility and generosity.

Accountability: We believe that each person is responsible for themselves and their happiness. Things happen to each one of us on our journeys and we alone choose how we respond. Ultimately, each of us is responsible for our actions.

Humility: Regardless of our family name, wealth, looks, skills, or intelligence, we are all creatures of God. We are all equally valuable in God's eyes. Remember to be humble at all times.

Generosity: We have each been blessed in many ways. Ultimately, we will be judged not by what we have accumulated but by what we have given away. We encourage you to demonstrate your gratitude for your gifts by being generous with both your time and your treasure.

It is our hope that when we are gone, we will have lived up to our obligations as parents and passed our core values on to you. Ultimately, we will measure the success of our legacy plan by whether we have accomplished the following goals.

1. We live our final years with purpose—giving and sharing with others.

2. We encourage you to be accountable for yourselves; humble and generous with those around you.

3. You receive your financial inheritance not with a sense of entitlement, but rather with a sense of stewardship.

4. We create opportunities for you to work and grow together through family meetings and charitable giving.

5. We are role models in how we have shared our wealth with those less fortunate and leave this world a better place.

Love,

Mom and Dad

Why We Established Trusts For You

Many beneficiaries mistakenly believe that their parents "lock up" their inheritance in trusts because their parents don't trust them. This letter explains that parents set up trusts because they love their children and want the trust to lessen the burden of sudden money.

llllllllllllllllllllllllllllllllllllllllllllllllllllllllllllllllllllllllllllllllllllllllllllllllllllllll

Dear children,

Since you are already mature, responsible adults, you may be surprised to learn that we put the bulk of your inheritance in trust for you. We want to explain our logic.

- Creditor Protection: We live in a litigious society and people with wealth are often sued. A trust will protect the assets for your benefit.

- Privacy: A trust provides a certain amount of protection from those who would prey on people coming into sudden wealth.

- Administration: The trustee will keep track of the assets, file tax returns and handle any legal requirements.

- Management: Pooling your assets under the management of a single trustee, at least initially, will yield economies of scale. Trustees are "fiduciaries" and must invest the assets solely for your benefit. It is our hope that the trustee will also act as a mentor to you, helping you gain confidence in money management, expenses, taxation, etc. Having a huge sum of money simply dumped on you with no direction can be overwhelming. A professional trustee can help you integrate the new wealth into your life, so it is less disruptive to you.

- Multigenerational: You may choose to pass all or a portion of your inheritance to your children and/or grandchildren. Under current tax law, having the property in trust allows you to do so without incurring additional estate taxes.

· Flexibility: Finally, these trusts have been drafted to provide you protection and the flexibility to meet your individual needs.

In an accompanying "Letter of Instruction" to the trustee, you will gain clearer insight on how we intend these trusts to be administered.

Love,

Mom and Dad

Our Family Meeting Fund

Too often when the second parent dies, children drift apart. Without the common bond of "Mom and Dad," children unintentionally fall out of the habit of getting together on a regular basis. This letter expresses the parents' hope that their children will continue to gather as a family unit and removes any financial obstacle to doing so.

Dear children,

When we are young, it is easy to take family for granted and pay little attention to nurturing relationships. As we grow older, however, we realize that families can easily fracture due to hurt feelings, perceived wrongs and/or simply inattention. From our perspective (now in the last third of life), we can confidently say, "Family is everything!"

As you know, we have been holding organized family meetings for a number of years.

Our goals have been consistent:

1. Build stronger personal relationships among each other so we can work better together when we are called upon to make difficult family decisions.

2. Share our personal values with you.

3. Share some aspects of our financial and estate plans with you.

4. Help educate you about finances and personal wealth building.

When we are both gone, we would like you to continue these meetings. In doing so, you honor us and our efforts to build a strong family. To that end, we have set aside a sum of money to create a limited liability company (LLC) to help pay for future family meetings. It is our hope that by subsidizing your meeting expenses, you will continue the tradition of family meetings long after we are gone.

In addition to subsidizing your meeting expenses, we believe that there is enough money set aside to pay a good portion of the cost of annual family reunions. Again, we hope you will continue hosting family reunions for yourselves and the generations that follow. We can only provide the structure and the funds: The implementation is up to you.

Love,

Mom and Dad

Why We Included Charitable Giving In Our Legacy Plan

The last thing parents want is for their children to resent that their parents left money to charity that might otherwise have gone to them. This letter explains why parents chose to make charitable bequests, and that they hope their children will also find joy in helping others.

|||||||||||||||||||||||||||||||||||||||||||||||||||||||||||||||||||||||||||||||||||||||||||||||||||||||||||||||||||||||||||||||||||||||||||||||||||

Dear children,

We have been extraordinarily blessed throughout our lifetimes. We have enjoyed good health; happy, healthy children and grandchildren; a loving extended family; fulfilling careers; and financial abundance.

In addition to making small financial gifts to you throughout your lives, we have bequeathed you enough of an inheritance to provide you financial security in your retirement. With the balance of our funds, we plan to help others.

During our lives we have shared with those less fortunate and intend to continue doing so after we are gone. Our giving through our estate plan will take three forms:

1. Deposit of a set sum into each of your own donor advised funds. You may distribute funds to organizations that are meaningful to you. For those of you with your own children, the donor advised fund could provide you the opportunity to instill in them the giving habit.

2. Deposit of a set sum in our donor advised fund. Our fund will provide you the opportunity to work together by continuing our work of supporting causes within our community.

3. Gifts to a couple of organization that have been particularly meaningful to us over many years. We will express our gratitude by leaving them an "ultimate" gift of the residual of our estate.

We may change the amounts and/or organizations, but as we write this letter, these are our intentions.

We have always felt that our ability to share with those less fortunate is a privilege and are humbled to have the opportunity. Thank you for continuing our tradition of giving. We hope you find it to be as rewarding as we have.

Love,

Mom and Dad

What You Can Expect To Receive From Our Legacy Plan

If you decide to share your letters with children, share this one last because it spells out—in dollar amounts—what each child will receive from your estate. Typically, this information is not provided to children until parents have met with them several times and feel their children are mature enough to handle the information responsibly. Alternatively, you can ask your advisors to share this letter with your children only after you die. (You might ask your advisors to review this letter to make certain that it is consistent with your legal documents.)

‖‖

Dear children,

With the letters and explanations that accompany this one, we have attempted to describe how our estate plan will work and why we made the choices we did. Exact dollar amounts may change based on the time of our deaths and change in value of our assets. At this time, however, you may each expect to receive the following upon our deaths.

1. Personal Property: You will receive all our personal property and may decide among yourselves how to equitably divide it.

2. Outright: You will each receive $_____ in cash shortly after the estate settles.

3. Trust: A trust will be established for each of you in the amount of $_____ with the intent to provide financial security for you in your retirement years.

4. Education: A sum of $_____ will be put in 529 Plans for each of our grandchildren.

5. Family LLC: A limited liability company will be formed upon our deaths, funded with $_____ to help offset the cost of future family meetings and reunions.

6. Individual donor advised accounts: A deposit of $_____ will be added to each of your accounts through our donor advised fund to make charitable grants to the nonprofits you choose.

7. Donor advised fund: A deposit of $_____ will be made to our donor advised fund for you to work together to make charitable grants to our community pursuant to our Charitable Giving Plan.

We share this with you now so you know what financial resources each of you can expect to receive upon our deaths and might incorporate this information into your own financial plans. While we always reserve the right to adjust our plans, we do not anticipate making any significant changes without discussing them with you. Please do not disclose this information or attempt to obtain credit by pledging these assets. We appreciate your discretion and trust your good judgment.

Love,

Mom and Dad

SECTION 2: LETTERS TO OTHERS

This section includes:

1. Letter To Our Trustee

2. Our Charitable Giving Plan

3. Letter Of Intention To Our Community Foundation

4. Educational Letter To Our Grandchildren

Letter To Our Trustee

The foundation of most all well-drafted estate plans is a trust. It is common in large, multi-generation estates that around 90% of a family's wealth is held in trust. Yet, when asked the question "Do you feel that the trusts of which you are a beneficiary are more a burden or blessing?" around 80% of the respondents choose burden. Wait…What?

You read that correctly. In the remarkably insightful book, Family Trusts, A Guide for Beneficiaries, Trustees, Trust Protectors, and Trust Creators *authors Hartley Goldstone, James Hughes and Keith Whitaker point out that most trusts are crafted primarily to avoid taxes, maintain grantor control, and protect beneficiaries from creditors. These trusts merely transfer assets from the parent's balance sheet to the child's balance sheet. Often, when heirs receive their inheritance in trust, they think "Dad didn't trust me!" or "He's still trying to control me from the grave!" On the other hand, true "gifts with spirit" are made freely and received freely.*

This letter is designed to 1) convey to a trustee the spirit of your gift, and 2) share with your children your reasons for establishing a trust.

Dear Trustee,

Thank you for serving as trustee for our children. It is our hope that the relationship will be mutually beneficial to both you and our children.

After reading our trust documents and the accompanying letters, you will soon realize our estate plan is quite different from the plans of most clients with whom you work. A Roman philosopher, Seneca, stated, "The manner in which a gift is given determines the manner in which it is received." It is our experience that many, if not most, people leave money in trust in an attempt to prevent their children from becoming spendthrifts. In other words, to protect children from themselves.

That is not our situation nor our intent. Our children are mature adults who have proven themselves to be financially responsible.

We trust their judgement. However, none of them has education or experience in managing large sums of money. While our trust documents set out "standards" (health, education, maintenance, support) for distribution, it is our wish that you be liberal in interpreting those standards. We want you to act more as a "mentor" than "gatekeeper."

Each child has his/her own trust and unique family situation. One may determine to consume the trust assets in their retirement years while another may wish to preserve and grow the assets for their heirs. Yet another may wish to gift portions of their assets to charity. Please work with each child closely to understand their personal situation and intentions and take time to teach them about money management and alternatives to achieve their goals. While we desire the protection a trust provides (attacks by creditors, bankruptcy, divorce, chemical dependence, incapacity, etc.), we expect your relationship to be one of collaboration with each beneficiary.

Throughout our adult lives we have worked closely with professional advisors who understand our intentions regarding our estate plan and our family. It is our hope that you will continue to work with these advisors.

Lastly, thank you for accepting this responsibility and for implementing it in the spirit of helping our children each achieve self-fulfillment.

Sincerely,

Our Charitable Giving Plan

Technically, this letter is not a letter, but a statement of purpose for your own use. You can share it with others or not. If you decide to share it with your children, it can highlight your values and act as a teaching tool.

||||||||||||||||||||||||||||||||||||||||||||||||||||||||||||||||||||||||||||||||||||||||||||||||||||||||||||||||||

The following self-reflection is meant to serve as the guide for our charitable giving journey. We intend to be purposeful rather than simply reactive. By targeting our gifts to organizations that align with our values, we hope to have a measurable positive impact on them while being a personally gratifying experience for us.

We acknowledge that not all our giving will fall within our desired parameters. For example, when a co-worker or neighbor asks us to support their child's school's fundraiser, we do. However, it is our intention to align most of our giving with the following values and parameters.

Why are we giving a portion of our resources to charities?

- **Gratitude:** We want to express our gratitude for the extraordinary blessings in our lives by giving to those less fortunate.

- **Responsibility:** "To whom much is given, much will be required" (Luke 12:48). We plan to use the wealth, wisdom, talents, and time we have been given to benefit others.

- **Rewarding:** Making a meaningful gift to another and witnessing the joy it can bring is personally very rewarding. Giving, in a sense, is a gift to ourselves.

What do we hope to accomplish?

- **Change:** We hope to improve the lives of others.

- **Fulfillment:** We hope to experience joy and a sense of personal fulfillment in working together to better our community.

- **Inspiration:** We hope to set an example for our children and grandchildren and inspire them to give freely to others in need.

What values will guide us?

We expect that most of our giving will be to organizations serving youth. Young people have a long time horizon, so impacting them in their formative years could have a multi-generational effect. Values that will guide us include:

- **Integrity:** We hope to help teach others to be true to themselves and to others in all their dealings.

- **Determination:** We hope our giving inspires recipients to work hard, stay focused, and never quit in the pursuit of a worthy goal.

- **Knowledge:** Education is a key to success in our society. We intend to support organizations that inspire learning.

Who will join us in our giving?

We do not have enough resources to make large scale changes in our community, much less the world. By collaborating with others and pooling our resources we believe our giving can be more effective.

- **Individuals:** We will look for opportunities to join other individuals or small groups to give our time, money, and energy to causes for which we share a passion.

- **Organizations:** Most of our giving will be to established organizations that have a proven record in delivering services to those in need.

- **Family:** We hope to pool assets with our children and work together toward achieving common goals.

What are some of the parameters that will guide us?

- **Geography:** We plan to focus our giving in our hometown where we have spent our lives and built our wealth.

- **Focus:** We will favor those organizations that work with youth promoting education, leadership development, healthy lifestyle, and good citizenship.

- **Personal Involvement:** We will designate a proportionately larger amount of funds to those few organizations where we volunteer our time and leadership abilities.

- **Capital Campaigns:** We plan to give modestly to capital campaigns and focus instead on annual gifts to support operations.

- **Pledges:** We prefer not to tie up our resources in multi-year pledges and focus instead on annual gifts that support operations.

- **Number of Organizations:** Spreading our resources over too many nonprofits will mean our gifts will have little to no effect on any of them. Rather, we plan to give to no more than four or five organizations in any one year so the results of our giving might be measurable.

- **Public Acknowledgment:** We will lend our name to our gifts where we feel it may encourage others to give. In circumstances we feel that is not the case, we will give anonymously.

- **Established Organizations:** We will be most comfortable giving to those nonprofits that have been serving the community for a number of years and have professional, proven leadership.

What will our giving budget be?

It is our intention that any gifts in excess of $_____ will come from either our donor advised fund or our IRA. We plan to spend our donor advised fund down over our lifetimes leaving only a small amount at the time of our last death. We will also begin making Qualified Charitable Distributions from our IRA. While we will review our finances each year, we estimate we can give up to $_____ per year.

How will we include our children?

We have written a letter to our children regarding our charitable giving. Each year at our Family Meeting we will discuss with them the organizations we contributed to and why.

We have established small donor advised funds for each child at our local community foundation. We plan to continue to transfer money from our donor advised fund each year to their donor advised funds from which they may make grants as they deem appropriate.

At our annual Family Meeting each child will be asked to report on their charitable giving including which organizations they selected; why; how much money they distributed; and what impact they achieved.

We anticipate keeping a record annually and cumulatively of the organizations the family contributed to as well as the amount of money given.

Upon our deaths, we have designated our donor advised fund to receive 100% of the balance in our IRA. We have filed a Letter of Intent to that effect with the community foundation.

Our goals upon our deaths are:

1. Provide a fund each child can use as a philanthropic teaching tool to make distributions with their own children.

2. Provide a fund that our children must agree on how to distribute each year at their Family Meeting.

3. Leave a final, "ultimate" gift, in our memory to a few of our favorite organizations.

How will we measure the success of our plan?

- **Tracking:** We will keep a spreadsheet of organizations that we gave to as a family that will include the dollar amount and date of each gift.

- **Impact:** We will regularly follow up with the nonprofits to measure the impact of our gifts as well as review the organization's mission, financial reports, and leadership.

- **Family:** We will gauge our children's level of engagement, solicit their feedback, and measure their level of satisfaction.

- **Fun:** Ultimately, it is a privilege to be able to give away money.

We want to have FUN with our Charitable Giving Plan and guard against it becoming a burden.

Letter of Intention
To Our Community Foundation

Many people make charitable bequests to a donor advised fund (DAF) at their local community foundations. DAFs can have a commercial sponsor or be a private foundation. It doesn't matter who the sponsor is. What matters is that you leave clear instructions as to how you want your charitable dollars deployed. When combined with your own Charitable Giving Plan and any letters to your children, the charitable fund sponsor will be able to administer your charitable dollars in a manner consistent with your intentions.

This letter is not legally binding. It can be changed by you at any time. By providing your community foundation (or DAF sponsor or private foundation, etc.) a current letter of instruction, you can minimize confusion upon your death and gain confidence that your wishes will be carried out.

Dear Sir/Madam:

Please read this letter in conjunction with our Charitable Giving Plan and our letter to our children explaining why we have included charity in our planning. Both are enclosed.

Upon both of our deaths, a significant sum of money, in accordance with our revocable trust and beneficiary designations, will be paid to our existing donor advised fund (DAF). You are directed to make lump-sum distributions from our DAF to the organizations in accordance with our written pledges. They are as follows:

$ _____   ABC Charity

$ _____   DEF Charity

$ _____   XYZ Charity

$ _____   Total

Next, $_____$ should be transferred to a DAF in the name of each of our children ($_____$ cumulatively). They should each have the sole right to direct grants from their individual funds.

Next, an amount up to $_____$ should be left in our existing DAF. We have set this up as an endowed fund so a deceased child's heir can succeed her/him. Decisions should be made by majority vote. Grant distributions should be limited to our hometown pursuant to the terms contained in our Charitable Giving Plan.

All remaining funds in our DAF should be distributed as follows:

	ORGANIZATION	PURPOSE
50%	His *alma mater*	student scholarships
50%	Her *alma mater*	student scholarships

We have chosen you as the sponsor of our DAF and the DAFs you will establish for our children, because you are acutely aware of the needs of our community. We want our charitable dollars to be spent in the community in which we raised our family and built our business.

Please help our children, upon their request, develop their own individualized Charitable Giving Plans. Allow our children to direct the funds in their own DAFs to whatever charitable organization and community they choose. We would also like you to help them use our DAF as a teaching tool for our grandchildren when appropriate. It is our hope that our children and grandchildren will work together for the betterment of our community.

Thank you for your guidance in helping our children and grandchildren become compassionate, intentional philanthropists.

Educational Letter To Our Grandchildren

Over the years, I have encouraged many individuals to help pay for their children's and grandchildren's college tuition with tax-favored dollars through Internal Revenue Service Code Section 529 (or "529 Plans"). Whether funding a four-year college or a trade school, these plans can be a great way to jumpstart a child's career.

Unfortunately, I've too often seen children (or grandchildren) view 529 Plans as a financial transaction. In that light, it's understandable that they feel a sense of entitlement. Accompanied by a personal letter from a parent or grandparent, however, a gift to a 529 Plan might be more meaningful and the receiver more grateful. A letter might even motivate a child or grandchild to work harder to make Grandma and Grandpa proud! Like "Why We Established Trusts for You," the purpose of this letter is to convey the spirit of the gift.

⸻

Dear grandchildren,

It is hard for us to believe that you will be graduating from high school and are proud of you and your accomplishments. We understand that you plan to attend college. While many people your age feel it is their "right" to attend college, that was not always the case. It was a privilege for a select few. As you prepare for this next chapter of your life, we want you to know how we would like to help.

Did you know the term "school" comes from a Greek word that means "free time?" School was a reward or an honor that was bestowed upon a young person who was allowed to spend some time thinking, learning and being introduced to new ideas rather than working in the fields all day.

Education is a life-long process that doesn't end when we graduate from high school (or college). On the contrary, our real education begins when we leave school, which is why the graduation ceremony is called a "commencement."

We were the first in our families to attend college. Rather than go to college, both of our fathers went directly into the military and our mothers were expected to get jobs. Very few women were allowed to continue their education back then. When our parents gave us the opportunity to attend college and offered to help pay part of our tuition, we each jumped at the chance! College was a wonderful experience. Not only did we learn about the world, but it is where we first met and fell in love!

When your father and his brother graduated from high school, we helped them pay part of their college tuition. We did not have enough to pay all of it, so they each worked part-time jobs and took out some student loans. They each worked hard and exceled in school. We think the fact they had to pay part of their tuition made them appreciate the value of school even more.

Since you were born, we have been putting money into a "529 Plan College Savings Account" for you hoping this day would come. As you know, college tuition, room and board can be very expensive. Many students graduating from high school simply cannot afford to go on to college. Others attend parttime so they can work fulltime to pay their tuition. It is our hope that the funds that we provide, combined with those of your parents', and your own work, will enable you to go to a school of your choice. Ideally, you will graduate with little debt.

As the third consecutive generation, to attend college, you are now part of a new family tradition. Please keep us apprised of your progress. We are excited for you as you start this new adventure!

Love,

Grandma and Grandpa

SECTION 3: WORKSHEETS FOR YOU AND YOUR ADVISORS

Throughout this book I have shared stories of how many affluent parents struggle with how much wealth to pass to their children. They want to find the amount that will enable their children to flourish without sapping their ambition or dulling their sense of self-worth. But how do they arrive at that right dollar amount?

The following four worksheets provide a methodology to find the dollar amount that is right for you and your children.

1. Why We Choose to Leave Money to Our Children

2. How We Chose Our Inheritance Amount

3. How We Would Like Our Children to Use Their Inheritance

4. The Values We Hope to Pass to Our Children

WHY WE CHOOSE TO LEAVE MONEY TO OUR CHILDREN

Leaving our property to our children is a choice, not a requirement. Using this worksheet, we articulate to ourselves why we wish to leave property to our children and what we hope to accomplish.

Most estate planning presupposes that parents want to leave assets to their children upon their deaths. Leaving assets, however, is a choice. Under the law, you may leave your assets to any individual, institution, or entity you choose. If you do not have living children or choose not to leave them assets upon your death(s), please so indicate below. If you have living children (and /or grandchildren), however, and you intend to leave a portion of your estate to them, please articulate the three or four specific reasons you have chosen to do so. If you are married, it is important to complete this worksheet as a couple.

❑ We do not have living children or do not want our assets to pass to them.

❑ We want to leave a portion of our wealth to our children for the following reasons. In order of priority these reasons include:

1. _____

2. _____

3. _____

4. _____

Note: This form has no legal binding effect. Your advisors may use it to trigger thought, discussion, and dialogue as they work to create a Legacy Plan for you.

Name_____

Date _____

How We Chose Our Inheritance Amount

Many, if not most, traditional estate plans pass to children "whatever is left" after paying taxes, expenses, and completing specific bequests. This method gives little thought to how parents want children to use the money, or how well-prepared children are to receive a sizeable inheritance. This worksheet fills that gap.

Complete this form only after you have answered the questions on Why We Choose To Leave Money To Our Children.

||||||||||||||||||||||||||||||||||||||||||||||||||||||||||||||||||||||||||||||||||||||||||||||||||||||||||||||||||||||||||||||||||||||||||||||

1. We believe that our combined estates will be worth about $ _____ upon our deaths.

2. We would like to leave our children an amount of as much as $ _____ upon our deaths.

You can express this number as a flat amount or as a percentage of your total estate if you prefer. You can include a "not to exceed" instruction to the amount. You can adjust the amount for inflation or state a set, unchanging amount. If you desire, you can state different amounts or percentages for each child or treat all children the same. Use the space below to describe your intentions.

3. We chose this amount because:

_____

_____

_____

Mark all statements that apply and provide explanations, if appropriate.

❑ The amount should be enough to achieve most or all of the items (listed on our *How We Would Like Our Children To Use Their Inheritance* worksheet) that we'd like to provide for our children.

❑ We think that we will have enough left in our estate at our deaths to provide this amount without affecting our retirement income needs.

❑ We believe that this inheritance amount will not affect our ability to make the charitable bequests we desire.

❑ It is our understanding that we can leave this inheritance to our children without adverse tax consequences.

❑ We will develop (or have already developed) a plan to help educate our children on how to handle an inheritance of this size in accordance with our values.

❑ It is our understanding that we can use trusts (or other entities) to protect our children's inheritance from creditors and predators.

❑ _____

_____

_____

_____

_____

_____

Names_____and_____

Date _____

*Note: While this form is designed to help you be purposeful in the distribution of your assets upon your death, **it has no legal, binding effect.** Your advisors will use it to initiate dialogue with you in the development of a legacy plan customized to meet your specific goals.*

How We Would Like Our Children
To Use Their Inheritance

This worksheet provides a practical, easy way for parents to agree on how they'd like their children to use the assets they leave. Not only will this information be particularly helpful to your advisors, but it can be a wonderful tool to initiate a conversation with your children.

The purpose of this worksheet is to help you make decisions about how you want your children to use the money you will leave and communicate your wishes to them. Both spouses should agree on the approximate amounts. While you cannot mandate how your children actually spend the money, this exercise will help you calculate an approximate amount that is comfortable for you. You may also use this worksheet to clarify and communicate your values to your children at the appropriate time.

Check the items that reflect your intentions and add others as you desire. Use the blank lines to add your thoughts, comments, or explanations.

We would feel good about our children using the inheritance they may receive from us to:

❏ Further their (or their children's) education.

Range: $_____

❏ Pay off debt.

Range: $_____

❏ Be able to retire at normal retirement age and live their final years self-sufficiently.

Range: $_____

❏ Purchase a bigger home.

Range: $_____

❑ Start or acquire a business.

Range: $_____

❑ Create an emergency fund.

Range: $_____

❑ Purchase a vacation home.

Range: $_____

❑ Start an investment fund.

Range: $_____

❑ Collect art, jewelry, sports cars, etc.

Range: $_____

❑ Help those less fortunate through gifts to charity.

Range: $_____

❑ Other use

Range: $_____

❑ Other use

Range: $_____

Additional comments: _____

_____

_____

Names (parents) _____   _____

The Values We Hope To Pass To Our Children

This worksheet will take some time and thought on your part. It should be completed separately by each spouse if you are married. By adding a comment after each value you select, you will clarify how you define the value for you personally. This will become your "true north" when faced with decisions throughout the planning process.

Our "legacy" is not simply the money we leave to nonprofit organizations in our community. We believe that our greatest legacy is our children and the impact that they will have on making this world a better place to live. Through both example and effort we have made in the past—and will make during our family meetings—we hope to pass on our values.

||||||||||||||||||||||||||||||||||||||||||||||||||||||||||||||||||||||||||||||||||||||||||||||||||||||||||||||||||||||

List three or four of the following values that are important to you, prioritize them, and write your comments describing how you interpret each value and/or how you want your children to live them out. Ideally, if you are married, you will mutually agree on your joint values.

VALUES

Abundance	Financial	Love
Acceptance	Independence	Loyalty
Accountability	Fitness	Modesty
Achievement	Forgiveness	Patience
Appreciation	Frugality	Perseverance
Commitment	Generosity	Pride
Compassion	Gratitude	Productivity
Competence	Health	Recognition
Contribution	Honesty	Respect
Courage	Honor	Responsibility
Dependability	Humility	Restraint
Determination	Independence	Sacrifice
Discipline	Integrity	Self-Control
Education	Intelligence	Self-Reliance
Empathy	Involvement	Self-Respect
Ethics	Justice	Sharing
Excellence	Kindness	Success
Fairness	Knowledge	Trustworthiness
Faith	Leadership	Wisdom

Some examples:

VALUE	YOUR COMMENTS
Hard work	Hard work is a gift. It builds self-esteem and self-reliance.
Integrity	We want our children to always "do the right thing," especially when no one is watching.
Gratitude	We have been given many blessings. We must be thankful through our words and actions.
Modesty	Each of us is equal in God's eyes. Be humble.

VALUE	YOUR COMMENTS
_____	_____
	_____
	_____
	_____
_____	_____
	_____
	_____
	_____

CHAPTER 9

Will You Accept The Responsibility Of Wealth?

The meaning of life is to find your gift.
The purpose of life is to give it away.
PABLO PICASSO

I see myself as an observer rather than an expert in legacy planning, so I have cited empirical studies and authors far more knowledgeable than myself throughout this book. I am not uber-wealthy or the product of multi-generational wealth like some of the individuals in my stories, yet I have more than I need, and have an incredibly rich family life.

What I am is a student and a teacher. I watch and absorb what is useful and discard the rest. I have learned the lessons in this book from working with affluent clients over decades, personally interviewing dozens of philanthropists, and engaging with highly accomplished students in the CAP® classes I have facilitated for a decade. To generate a process and discipline my own thinking I created the worksheets in the previous chapter. The letters are based on letters my wife and I wrote to our children. The suggestions for conducting effective family meetings are not theoretical. Instead, they are a result of trial and error with my own family, so I know what does and does not work. I encourage you to download the worksheets and letters *(SpectrumOfLegacies.com)*, modify them, improve on them, personalize them, and make them your own.

Having recently retired from a rewarding 40-year career in financial services, I plan to devote the next phase of my life to teaching families and advisors some of the lessons I have learned. I will facilitate CAP® classes; teach my own children to be good stewards of money; volunteer time; and give financial resources to nonprofits in my community. In short, I will be working on my own legacy.

I will consider this book to be a success if you acknowledge and accept that with the blessings of wealth come responsibility, and you commit to at least one action that will enhance your legacy. You now have the tools (forms, worksheets, and letters) and a spectrum of legacies to choose from.

· Talk to your children.

· Write them letters.

· Start holding family meetings.

· Prepare a personal charitable giving plan.

· Include a charitable bequest in your estate plan.

· Increase your current charitable giving.

The rewards to you, your family and community for creating a legacy are many and measurable.

· When you develop a plan based on your core values, you will feel a genuine sense of self-fulfillment in addition to relief.

· You and your children will learn to communicate better, trust each other more, and grow closer as a family.

· Your children will be better prepared to handle money, have more confidence they are acting as you would want them to, and more likely to feel that they are stewards of the money entrusted to them.

· Making lifetime gifts to charity in accordance with your values, pursuant to your own personalized giving plan will increase your sense of happiness, help you live longer and help you accumulate more net worth by the time of your death.[8]

---

[8]*Charitable estate planning and subsequent wealth accumulation: Why percentage gifts may be worth more than we thought* by Russell N. James, III, JD, PhD International Journal of Educational Advancement Vol. 10.1, 24-32

· You will live the last years of your life in a state of abundance, confident that you have done all you can for your family and community, all the while earning their respect.

It is my sincere desire that you will take the lessons from this book and apply them to your own family. If we all accept the responsibilities of wealth and work together, we can build closer families, healthier communities, and meaningful personal legacies. After all, it's your life, your family, your LEGACY!

Be the change you want to see in the world.
MAHATMA GANDHI

ACKNOWLEDGMENTS

I thank my wonderful wife, Tricia, for her patience and unrelenting support. Without her encouragement and love, this book would not have become a reality.

My children and their spouses have been the recipients of many of the ideas and techniques described in this book. Their real-time feedback has been invaluable. I am grateful for their patience and good-natured input. They have given me confidence that they will be good stewards of their eventual inheritance and be generous contributors to their communities.

My editor, Kathy Bolinske, has been a tremendous asset. Writing a book is more complex and tedious than I anticipated, and most readers appreciate. Kathy's sense of humor, astute observations and steady hand made her an invaluable and fun partner in this endeavor.

Professor Phil Cubeta continues to lead the Chartered Advisor in Philanthropy® (CAP®) designation program at The American College of Financial Services. His steadfast support of me, the Omaha CAP® study group program, and the writing of this book, have meant everything to me. His friendship is something I cherish.

John A. Warnick's work at the Purposeful Planning Institute has been a consistent source of fresh ideas and resources for this book. I thank John for quietly changing an entire industry through his persistent, humble leadership.

It was Warren Buffett's example that motivated me to embark on this ten-year journey of facilitating CAP® classes in Omaha and writing two books. He truly "walks the talk!" I thank him for his leadership, inspiration, and encouragement.

I also thank the over 130 graduates of the Omaha CAP® Study Group program who believed they could make a difference and have done exactly that. Through their efforts, this grand experiment of sorts has made Omaha a more generous community—$9 billion in charitable gifts and bequests to date.

My gratitude goes to George Nichols, President and CEO of The American College of Financial Services, who has been an enthusiastic supporter of the CAP® program. To spread this book's message to as many people as possible, he personally funded the College's *A Spectrum of Legacies* self-paced, online course.

Finally, thank you to the many families that read my first book, *The Legacy Spectrum*, and subsequently shared with me heartwarming stories of how they are passing their values to their children through family meetings, letters and giving together as a family. They are making a positive impact on their families and their communities today and for generations to come.

ABOUT THE AUTHOR

Mark A. Weber is the founder of Legacy Spectrum Advisor, LLC and has provided financial and estate planning advice to wealthy families for over 40 years. He has led scores of advisors through philanthropy classes that have benefitted hundreds of families, nonprofits, and communities. In his own family, he has helped two generations create meaningful legacies and build closer family ties.

You can learn more about Mark at *SpectrumOfLegacies.com/author* or dive deeper into legacy planning through The American College of Financial Services' free course, A Spectrum of Legacies, *http://knowledge. theamericancollege.edu/acton/media/1564/a-spectrum-of-legacies-cd*.

MARK'S BOOKSHELF

If you have enjoyed reading this book and would like to learn more about Legacy / Purposeful / Values-driven planning, here are some of my favorite books.

Preparing Heirs: Five Steps to a Successful Transition of Family Wealth and Values by Roy Williams and Vic Preisser, Robert Reed Publishers, 2010

The Right Side of The Table: Where Do You Sit in the Minds of the Affluent? by Scott and Todd Fithian, The Legacy Companies, 2007

Wealth in Families by Charles W. Collier, Harvard, 2nd edition, 2006

TrustWorthy: New Angles on Trusts from Beneficiaries and Trustees by Hartley Goldstone and Kathy Wiseman, Trustscape LLC, 2012

Family Trusts: A Guide for Beneficiaries, Trustees, Trust Protectors and Trust Creators by Hartley Goldstone, James E. Hughes, Jr, and Keith Whitaker, Wiley, 2015

The Cycle of the Gift: Family Wealth and Wisdom by James E. Hughes, Jr, Susan E. Massenzio, and Keith Whitaker, Bloomberg Press, 2012

Complete Family Wealth by James E. Hughes, Jr, Susan E. Massenzio, and Keith Whitaker, Bloomberg Press, 2017

Entrusted: Building a Legacy That Lasts by David R. York and Andrew L. Howell, YH Publishing, LLC, 2015

Riveted: 44 Values That Change The World by David R. York and Andrew L. Howell, Redwood Publishing, LLC, 2018

Silver Spoon Kids: How Successful Parents Raise Responsible Children, by Eileen Gallo, PhD and Jon J. Gallo, McGraw-Hill Education, 2002

Strangers In Paradise: How Families Adapt to Wealth Across Generations by James Grubman, Ph.D., FamilyWealth Consulting, 2013

Made in the USA
Middletown, DE
16 September 2023

38380730R00106